JLO Art of Cooking

Junior League of Ogden Cookbook

JUNIOR LEAGUE OF OGDEN
Women building better communities

2580 Jefferson Avenue
Ogden, Utah 84401-2493
(801) 393-2540
Fax (801) 392-5295
www.juniorleagueofogden.org

Library of Congress Number:
2003091929

ISBN: 0-9740100-0-6

Designed, Edited and
Manufactured by:

marketing & communications

A subsidiary of James & Co. Business Advisors / CPAs

3535 Lincoln Avenue
Ogden, Utah 84401
(801) 622-1212
www.designsolutionsllc.com

Designers: Bonie Shupe,
Cherie Hanson, Ryan Nisogi,
and Renee Froerer

Project Manager: Jodi Holmgren
Project Coordinator: Jeremy Holt

Cover Art by: Julie Lewis
Bindery by: Express Solutions

Manufactured in the
United States of America in the
State of Utah
First Printing: 2003
10,000 copies

Painting by: Debra Marin

Junior League of Ogden

OUR MISSION

Junior League of Ogden is an organization of volunteers who
work to improve the quality of life in their community and the
potential of women through training, leadership development
and support in an atmosphere of friendship.

The Association of Junior Leagues International Inc. is an
organization of women committed to promoting voluntarism,
developing the potential of women and improving
communities through the effective action and leadership of
trained volunteers. Its purpose is exclusively educational and
charitable.

OVER 50 YEARS OF SERVICE

The Junior League of Ogden (JLO) was founded in 1934 as
the Welfare League of Ogden. It joined the Association of
Junior Leagues International (AJLI) in 1953. Since its
inception, the Junior League of Ogden has been an advocate
for women and children's issues. Throughout its history,
League members have given generously of their time, talent
and resources to help build a better community.

Introduction

Junior League of Ogden (JLO) is a group of women who love their community and all it has to offer. From the Historic District and buildings commonly used as movie sets, to cultural and educational opportunities, Weber County and the city of Ogden are framed by scenic beauty and incredible outdoor recreation. Ogden is home to a world-class ski resort, which hosted several events in the 2002 Winter Olympics, as well as a venue that participates in the annual Sundance Film Festival.

As with many Junior Leagues, the Junior League of Ogden is made up of a diverse group of women. The recipes featured in this book reflect that diversity. Some recipes have come from members who have lived all over the country and have carried unique flavors with them. Others are local favorites that have been passed down from generation to generation.

With today's busy lifestyle, these recipes will compliment an evening of entertaining or provide a quick meal with ingredients readily available at the local grocery store. The wonderful fresh produce found at the downtown Ogden Farmers' Market or along the "Fruit Highway" are true favorites to many and are sure to enhance any recipe.

Proceeds from the sale of JLO Art of Cooking will be returned to the community through the training of volunteers and the development of community projects.

ON THE COVER

In the painting showcased on the cover of JLO Art of Cooking, the artist Julie Lewis depicts the four generation tradition of preparing their grandmother's recipe for "Pustard Mickles" (see page 22). The recipe requires two glorious fall days; one for chopping and brining vegetables, one for heating mustard sauce and filling the bottles. Friendship, poems and good pickles are the result! The artist's grandmother was Blanche Browning Rich and her mother, Sharon Lewis, is a sustainer of the Junior League of Ogden.

Table of Contents

Painting by: Steve Songer

*T*he Eccles Community Art Center is home to the offices of the Junior League of Ogden. The recently restored building, which dates from 1893, is listed on the National Register of Historic Places and is the only nonprofit art center in the greater Ogden area. In addition to its permanent art collection, the Main House and Carriage House Galleries host exhibits by local, regional and national artists. The new Renaissance Complex, home to ongoing educational programs and performing arts, features a beautiful sculpture garden with a fountain and seating areas. As a 50th anniversary commemorative gift to the community, Junior League of Ogden purchased a sculpture for the garden to represent their dedication to the health and welfare of children and the potential of women.

Painting by: Liz Pierce

Social dancing was a popular entertainment in the twentieth century, and Ogden's dance halls and ballrooms drew large crowds. The most frequented establishments were the Berthana Ballroom (above), the White City Ballroom and Weber College Dance Hall. On occasion, dance parties were also held at Union Station and in the Ben Lomond Hotel Ballroom.

APPETIZERS AND BEVERAGES

Avocado-Corn Salsa

1   (15 ounce) can whole kernel
     corn, drained
1   (15 ounce) can black beans,
     drained and rinsed
3   large tomatoes, diced
¹/₂ bunch cilantro, chopped
¹/₄ cup green onions, chopped
1   package dry Italian dressing
     jalapeños, diced - add to taste
2   avocados, diced

Prepare dressing according to directions on package. Add remaining ingredients except avocado and toss gently. (Can be prepared 8 hours ahead. Cover and refrigerate.) Just before serving, mix diced avocado into salsa. Season to taste with salt and pepper.

Yield: 2 ¹/₃ cups

Fresh Salsa

4   cloves garlic, sliced
2   teaspoons salt
4   tablespoons vegetable oil
4   tablespoons apple cider
     vinegar
2   tablespoons sugar
16 Roma tomatoes
2   sweet yellow onions
2   purple or red onions
2   orange bell peppers, seeded,
     diced
2   red bell peppers, seeded, diced
2   yellow bell peppers, seeded,
     diced
1   purple bell pepper (or green),
     seeded, diced
3   Anaheim chili peppers, diced
2   orange habanero chilies, diced

Peel and slice the garlic cloves, put in a bowl and cover with salt. Mash with a fork until it is a paste-like consistency. Add the oil, vinegar and sugar and mix well. Peel, core and dice tomatoes, onions and bell peppers (remove seeds). Do the same with chili peppers, but include seeds. Mix all ingredients together, except chilies. Add these to taste, depending on desired hotness.

Fruit Salsa

1 papaya, chopped
1 cup cucumber, diced
3 cloves garlic, minced
2 teaspoons fresh ginger, minced
1 fresh pineapple, drained and
   chopped
8 mint leaves, finely chopped
4 teaspoons fresh cilantro,
   chopped
juice of 2 lemons
$^1/_4$-$^1/_2$ teaspoon of chili pepper
$^1/_2$ sweet onion, chopped

Combine all ingredients. Make ahead of time so flavors blend together. Serve chilled.

Mango or Papaya Salsa

2 avocados, pitted, peeled, diced
1 firm-ripe medium mango or
   papaya peeled, seeded and
   finely diced (about 2 cups)
$^1/_2$ small red onion, finely
   chopped (about $^1/_4$ cup),
   soaked in cold water for 20
   minutes and drained
1 jalapeño, minced, or $^1/_2$
   teaspoon hot sauce
3 tablespoons fresh lime juice
2 tablespoons chopped fresh
   cilantro
$^1/_2$ teaspoon salt, or to taste

In a bowl, combine all ingredients in order, add salt to taste. Chill for at least 30 minutes before serving.

Suggestions: Serve with tacos, fish or chips.

Yield: approximately 2 cups

Artichoke Heart Dip

3   cans artichoke heart quarters, (packed in water), drained and chopped
8   ounces mayonnaise
8   ounces sour cream
1   package Hidden Valley Ranch Original Buttermilk Dressing® (dry mix)
cayenne pepper
squeeze of lemon

Thoroughly drain artichoke hearts (squeeze out all the water) and chop. Mix artichoke hearts, mayonnaise, sour cream and dry dressing mix. Add cayenne pepper to taste and a squeeze of lemon. (Best to prepare the night before.)

Serve with bagel chips, crackers or pita bread.

Hummus with Parsley-Pesto Oil

4   garlic cloves
1   teaspoon salt
1   (19 ounce) can chick-peas, drained and rinsed
$2/3$ cup well-stirred tahini
$1/4$ cup fresh lemon juice, or to taste
$1/2$ cup olive oil, or to taste
$1/4$ cup fresh parsley leaves, chopped
2   tablespoons pine nuts, toasted lightly

On a cutting board mince and mash the garlic to a paste with the salt. In a food processor purée the chick-peas, garlic paste, tahini, lemon juice, $1/4$ cup of the oil and $1/2$ cup water, scraping down the sides until hummus is smooth and add salt to taste. Add water, if necessary, to thin the hummus to the desired consistency. Transfer the hummus to a bowl. In the food processor, purée the remaining $1/4$ cup oil with the parsley until the oil is bright green and the parsley is minced, transfer the parsley oil to a small jar. Drizzle the hummus with the parsley oil and sprinkle it with the pine nuts.

Serve with toasted pita thins.

Tip: The hummus may be made up to 3 days in advance and kept covered and chilled.

Yield: 4 cups

Sheepherders' Dip

1   (10 ounce) package frozen or
    fresh spinach, chopped
2   cups sour cream
2   cups mayonnaise
1   package Knorr® Dry Vegetable
    Soup Mix
1   (8 ounce) can water chestnuts,
    drained and chopped

Combine all ingredients. Chill at least 2 hours before serving.

Serve in bread bowl.

Yield: 4 $\frac{1}{2}$ cups

Blue Ribbon Dip

8   ounces blue cheese, crumbled
2   cloves garlic, minced
$\frac{1}{2}$ cup olive oil
2   tablespoons red wine vinegar
1   tablespoon lemon juice
$\frac{1}{2}$ cup red onion, chopped
$\frac{1}{2}$ cup fresh parsley, minced
$\frac{1}{4}$ teaspoon black pepper

Combine all ingredients and spread onto shallow dish. Refrigerate at least 1 hour prior to serving.

Serve with baguette slices, crackers or fresh vegetables.

Yield: 1 $\frac{1}{2}$ cups

Dipping Oil

1   cup oil
$\frac{1}{2}$ cup balsamic vinegar
$\frac{1}{2}$ cup Parmesan cheese
$1\frac{1}{2}$ tablespoons dried basil
$\frac{1}{2}$ teaspoon pepper
$\frac{1}{2}$ teaspoon salt
4-5 cloves of garlic, minced

Mix and serve at room temperature. Can chill in refrigerator for up to one month.

Yield: 2 cups

Smoked Salmon Spread

8   ounces cream cheese, softened
     to room temperature
1/4 cup heavy cream
1   tablespoon fresh lemon juice
2-3 dashes of Tabasco®
1   teaspoon dried dill
1   large shallot, finely diced
1   green scallion, thinly sliced
1/4 pound smoked salmon, lightly
     shredded

Mix cream cheese, cream, lemon juice, Tabasco®, dill and shallots until smooth. Gently fold in scallions and salmon.

Garnish with lemon slices, fresh dill or scallion fans and serve with crackers.

Tip: Although this can be served immediately, it is really good if it is made several hours ahead or store in refrigerator day before serving to let flavors mellow together.

Servings: 2 cups

Chunky Guacamole

2   ripe avocados, peeled and
     pitted, chopped or mashed
2   cups plum tomatoes, seeded
     and chopped
1   cup cucumber, peeled, seeded
     and chopped
1/2 cup green onion, chopped
1/4 cup fresh lime juice
1/4 cup fresh cilantro, chopped
2   tablespoons jalapeño, seeded,
     minced
1   teaspoon salt
2   teaspoons garlic minced

Mix all ingredients together. Serve with chips.

Servings: 4

Warm Spinach Dip

1 tablespoon jalapeños, chopped

³/₄ cup onions, chopped

2 tomatoes, chopped (about 2 cups)

1 (10 ounce) package frozen spinach, thawed and squeezed dry

1 (8 ounce) package cream cheese, softened

2 cups Monterey Jack cheese, shredded

¹/₃ cup half-and-half

In medium bowl, mix all ingredients thoroughly together and pour into buttered oven-proof dish. Bake at 400 degrees for 20-25 minutes.

Serve warm with tortilla chips.

Servings: 8-10

Dining Car Special
RED APPLE CHEESE BALL

4 cups sharp Cheddar cheese, grated (approximately 1 pound of cheese)

1 (3 ounce) package cream cheese, softened

¹/₂ cup apple cider

1 teaspoon Worcestershire sauce

1 teaspoon dry mustard

¹/₂ teaspoon onion salt

¹/₄ teaspoon cayenne pepper

2 teaspoons caraway seeds

paprika

cinnamon stick

Combine cheeses, cider, seasonings and seeds; beat until smooth. Refrigerate 2-3 hours. Shape into a round, apple shaped ball. Roll all sides in paprika to create a "red apple." Insert cinnamon stick for stem. Refrigerate until served.

Serve as a spread with an assortment of sliced red and golden delicious apples and crackers.

Yield: 3 cups

Spinach Triangles

FILLING:

1 (10 ounce) package frozen chopped spinach, thawed

$^1/_2$ cup onion, chopped

1 clove garlic, minced

6 ounces feta cheese, finely crumbled

$^1/_2$ teaspoon dried oregano, crushed

TRIANGLES:

12 sheets phyllo dough (8-10 ounces)

$^1/_2$ cup margarine or butter, melted

To make filling: Cook spinach, onion and garlic according to spinach package directions. Drain well in colander. Press the back of a spoon against mixture to force out excess moisture. Combine spinach mixture, feta cheese and oregano.

Lightly brush 1 sheet of phyllo with some of the melted margarine or butter. Place another phyllo sheet on top; brush with some margarine. Repeat with a third sheet of phyllo and margarine. (Cover the remaining phyllo with a damp cloth to prevent drying.) Cut the stack of phyllo lengthwise into 6 strips.

For each triangle, spoon about 1 tablespoon of the filling about 1-inch from one end of each strip. Fold the end over the filling at a 45-degree angle. Continue folding to form a triangle that encloses filling. Repeat with remaining phyllo, margarine or butter and filling.

Place triangles on a baking sheet. Brush with margarine. Bake at 375 degrees for 18-20 minutes or until golden. Serve warm.

Yield: 24

Painting by: Scott Wallis

Hanky Panks

1   loaf party rye bread
1   pound ground beef
1   pound hot spicy sausage
1   pound Velveeta® cheese
$1/2$ teaspoon oregano
$1/2$ teaspoon garlic salt
$1/2$ tablespoon Worcestershire
      sauce

Brown ground beef and sausage together and drain. Melt cheese in skillet with meat. Add other ingredients. Stir until well blended. Spread on slices of party rye. Broil until mixture bubbles.

Tip: Can be spread on bread, placed on cookie sheets and frozen, then transferred to freezer containers for make-ahead appetizers.

Blue Cheese Log

6   ounces blue cheese ($1^1/2$ cups)
1   (3 ounce) package cream
     cheese, softened
$1/4$ cup sour cream
$1/2$ cup toasted walnuts, chopped
$1/2$ cup toasted walnuts, ground
2   pears, sliced
toasted baguette slices

Stir together blue cheese, cream cheese and sour cream. Stir in chopped walnuts. Cover and chill about 1 hour or until easy to handle. Divide mixture in half; shape each half into a 6x$1^1/2$-inch diameter log. Wrap in plastic wrap and chill at least 4 hours or until firm.

Place ground walnuts on a sheet of waxed paper. Roll log in walnuts. Wrap in plastic wrap and chill up to 24 hours.

Serve with pear slices and baguette slices. To make ahead: freeze wrapped logs up to 1 week.

Servings: 16-20

Sicilian Caponata

1   large eggplant, unpeeled
$^2/_3$ cup olive oil
2   medium onions, diced
1   cup diced celery
1   pound Italian tomatoes and juice
$^1/_3$ cup red wine vinegar
1   tablespoon sugar
2   teaspoons salt
$^1/_4$ teaspoon pepper
3   dashes cayenne pepper
1   (14 ounce) can green or ripe olives, diced
2   tablespoons capers with 1 tablespoon juice
2   tablespoons pine nuts
juice of one lemon

Cut eggplant into $^1/_2$-inch cubes. Heat $^1/_3$ cup olive oil in large skillet. Sauté eggplant for 5 minutes, stirring often. It will absorb oil and change color slightly; remove from heat. Add remaining oil to skillet and sauté onions until transparent. Add celery and tomatoes with liquid. Cook over medium heat about 15 minutes, stirring often until sauce has reduced and thickened. Stir in vinegar, sugar, seasonings and eggplant. Cook covered for 10 minutes. Add olives, capers and pine nuts and cook uncovered 10 minutes longer. Check seasonings and add lemon juice to taste. Chill well before serving. Make 24 hours in advance. Refrigerates well for 2 weeks and freezes well.

Serve on toasted French bread rounds.

Servings: 8

Layered Goat Cheese Appetizer

4 ounces plain goat cheese

olive oil

2 cloves garlic, minced

1 (4 ounce) jar oil packed
sun-dried tomatoes

$^{1}/_{2}$ cup fresh basil, chopped

$^{1}/_{4}$ cup pine nuts

Spread goat cheese on serving plate – drizzle olive oil on top and then spread minced garlic on top of that. Chop sun-dried tomatoes and add to the top. Next add chopped fresh basil and sprinkle with pine nuts.

Serve with crackers or bagel chips.

Marinated Cheese

$^{1}/_{2}$ cup olive oil

$^{1}/_{2}$ cup white wine vinegar

3 tablespoons fresh parsley,
chopped

3 tablespoons green onion,
minced

1 teaspoon sugar

$^{3}/_{4}$ teaspoon dried basil

$^{1}/_{2}$ teaspoon salt

$^{1}/_{2}$ teaspoon pepper

3 cloves garlic, minced

1 (2 ounce) jar diced pimento,
drained

1 (8 ounce) block sharp
Cheddar cheese, chilled

1 (8 ounce) block cream cheese,
chilled

Combine olive oil, vinegar, parsley, onion, sugar, basil, salt, pepper, garlic and pimento in a jar and shake vigorously. Set marinade aside.

Cut block of Cheddar in half lengthwise. Cut crosswise into $^{1}/_{4}$-inch-thick slices. Set aside. Repeat procedure with cream cheese. Stand cheese slices on edge in a shallow dish, alternating types of cheese. Pour marinade over cheese.

Garnish with fresh parsley sprigs.

Serve with assorted crackers.

Pete's Pâté

1 cup onions, diced
$^1/_2$ pound mushrooms, diced
1 stick butter
4 tablespoons olive oil
$1^1/_2$ cup stock with good flavor
  (chicken broth or veal stock)
1 cup red wine
$^1/_2$ cup sherry
2 cloves fresh garlic, finely
  minced
1 pound chicken livers (usually
  sold in 1 to 1.5 pound tubs,
  just use it all)
salt and pepper to taste
$^1/_3$ cup heavy cream

Finely dice onions and mushrooms. Heat a large skillet or braising pan and add 2 tablespoons of olive oil and 2 tablespoons of butter. Sauté mushrooms and onions stirring occasionally for 5 minutes. If they seem dry, add another tablespoon of butter or olive oil. Season with salt and pepper, cover with a lid to release some moisture from the mushrooms. Remove lid after 5 minutes and cook off moisture another 5 minutes. Add $^1/_2$ cup of stock, stir in and let reduce more.

Meanwhile, drain off liver and cut up a bit while removing the stringy vein in each lobe. (You can feel the hard vein with your fingers and dissect it out with a knife.) When onions and mushrooms are almost dry, add $^1/_4$ cup wine and cook until reduced. Then add $^1/_4$ cup sherry and cook until reduced.

Remove onions and mushrooms and any juices from the skillet and set aside. In the skillet, heat 1 tablespoon of olive oil and 2 tablespoons of butter. Sauté garlic for 2 minutes. Add liver and cook, breaking up any big chunks. Generously season with salt and pepper. After about 10 minutes, add $^1/_2$ cup stock, cook until liquid has evaporated. Add $^1/_4$ cup red wine and cook until reduced, then add $^1/_4$ cup sherry, then again with stock, then again with red wine. Cook the last time until mixture is fairly dry. Turn off heat and let cool.

Put onions, mushrooms and liver in a food processor. Pulse food processor off and on for 5 seconds at a time to purée. Blend in $^1/_3$ cup heavy cream; adjust salt and pepper.

Serve with crackers as a great appetizer. Serve immediately or store in refrigerator and several days later. This pâté also freezes well.

Yield: approximately 2 cups

Note: Making pâté is not an exact science, you will do several reductions of stock, wine and sherry with the onions, mushrooms and liver, then blend it together with a little cream.

Eggplant Caviar

1   large eggplant, cut in half
2   tablespoons olive oil
1/2   onion, chopped
2   large cloves garlic, minced
1/2   teaspoon salt
1/4   cup Italian parsley, chopped
1/2   red bell pepper, diced
juice of 1/2 lemon

Preheat oven to 350 degrees. Salt, pepper and lightly oil eggplant halves. Place eggplant on a baking sheet and bake for 45-60 minutes or until soft in center. Cool. Scrape eggplant flesh into a mixing bowl. In small skillet, heat olive oil. Add onion and garlic, saute until onion is soft. Place in mixing bowl with eggplant. Add salt, parsley, diced red pepper and lemon juice. Mix well, mashing eggplant until all ingredients are combined.

Serve at room temperature on crackers, toasted pita triangles or baguette toasts.

Note: This recipe is best made the night before serving to allow the flavors to meld.

Bruschetta

1   French baguette
4   roma tomatoes, chopped
1/2   red onion, chopped
1   clove of garlic, minced
2   tablespoons olive oil
2   tablespoons balsamic vinegar
2   tablespoons fresh basil, chopped
1/2   cup grated Parmesan cheese, for garnish

Mix tomatoes, onion, garlic, olive oil, vinegar and basil. Marinate for several minutes. Slice baguette into 1/2-inch thick rounds. Brush each round with olive oil. Toast in a preheated 350 degree oven on a baking sheet until slightly brown. Cool. Top each round with a spoonful of tomato mixture. Garnish with grated Parmesan.

Crab Cakes with Tarragon Aioli & Cabbage Salad

CABBAGE SALAD:

green cabbage thinly sliced ($1/2$ cup
    per person)
sea salt
fresh chives
white wine or champagne vinegar

TARRAGON AIOLI:

2   egg yolks
3   cloves of garlic
juice of 1 lemon
$1/2$ teaspoon salt
1   dash Tabasco® sauce
$1/4$ cup very hot water
2   cups olive oil
$1/2$ bunch tarragon, finely
    chopped

CRAB CAKES:

$1 1/2$ pounds Dungeness crab meat
$3/4$ cup panko bread crumbs plus
    additional for outer coating
    (from oriental market)
2   green onions, finely chopped
oil for sautéing

To make cabbage salad: Toss thinly sliced cabbage with sprinkling of salt and let stand in bowl 30 minutes. Drain off liquid from cabbage and add chives and vinegar to taste. Rinse salt off cabbage and thoroughly dry with paper towel prior to adding chives and vinegar.

Arrange cabbage on individual plates, put crab cakes on top and drizzle with aioli.

To make tarragon aioli: In a food processor or blender, place all ingredients up to and including Tabasco® and run the machine. Pour in hot water and process for 15 seconds. With machine running, slowly drizzle in oil until a mayonnaise consistency is reached. Stir in tarragon. Set aside (refrigerate).

To make crab cakes: Combine crab, bread crumbs and green onions. Add $1/2$ cup aioli and test mixture to see how well it holds together. If needed, add up to an additional $1/4$ cup aioli. Do not overcook ingredients. Cakes should be loose and just barely held together. Form into cakes about 3-inches in diameter (or smaller for appetizers) and place one side in bread crumbs.

Heat oil on medium-high heat until just smoking. Place cakes, bread crumb side down, in pan. Sauté until golden and carefully turn over. Lower heat to medium and sauté until heated through. Serve on cabbage salad and top with additional aioli.

Gingered Shrimp Toast

1   loaf sliced white bread
1   pound medium shrimp,
    peeled and deveined
1   small onion or 2 green onions,
    minced
1½ inch slice fresh ginger root,
    minced
1   tablespoon wine or sherry
½   teaspoon salt
¼   teaspoon pepper, ground
2   egg whites
vegetable oil for frying
fresh parsley sprigs for garnish
plum sauce (see below)

Remove crusts from bread and reserve. Cut each slice diagonally to form triangle. Process reserved bread crusts in food processor. Set aside ½ cup fine bread crumbs. Process next 6 ingredients in food processor until finely chopped. With motor running, pour in egg whites and process until well combined. Spread mixture ¼-inch thick on bread pieces. Dip mixture-coated sides in bread crumbs. Place on cookie sheet and cover with plastic wrap. Chill until time to fry. May be refrigerated 1 day or frozen 2 weeks. Do not thaw before frying.

Heat 1½-2-inches oil in large skillet over moderate heat. Fry toast in batches until golden brown on both sides. Drain on paper towels. Place on a large platter, garnish with parsley and serve with plum sauce (below).

Servings: 30 appetizers

Plum Sauce

1   (12 ounce) jar plum preserves
1   tablespoon vinegar
1   tablespoon brown sugar
1   tablespoon onion, finely
    chopped
1   teaspoon red pepper, crushed
1   clove garlic, minced
½   teaspoon ground ginger

In small saucepan combine all ingredients and bring to a boil, stirring constantly. Remove from heat, refrigerate. A great dipping sauce for gingered shrimp toast, deep-fried wontons or egg rolls.

Walnut Blue-Cheese Coins

1   cup toasted walnuts
    (3 $^1/_4$ ounces)
$^3/_4$ cup all-purpose flour, plus
    more for dusting
$^1/_2$ teaspoon salt
$^1/_4$ teaspoon pepper, freshly
    ground
$^1/_4$ teaspoon baking soda
2   tablespoons butter, cold,
    unsalted, cut in pieces
$^1/_4$ pound blue cheese, crumbled
coarse salt for sprinkling

In the bowl of a food processor, finely grind $^1/_2$ cup walnuts. Add flour, salt, pepper and baking soda; pulse to combine. Add butter; pulse until mixture resembles coarse meal. Add cheese; pulse until dough comes together, about 15 seconds.

Preheat oven to 350 degrees. Transfer dough to lightly floured surface; divide into 2 equal parts. Using your hands, roll dough into 2 (1$^1/_2$ -inch) logs. Coarsely chop remaining $^1/_2$ cup walnuts; sprinkle over a clean work surface. Roll logs in walnuts. Wrap each log in plastic wrap and chill until firm, at least 3 hours.

Slice logs into $^1/_4$-inch-thick coins. Transfer to ungreased baking sheet; sprinkle lightly with coarse salt. Bake until centers are firm to the touch, about 15 minutes. Transfer to a wire rack to cool. Store in an airtight container, at room temperature, 3-4 days.

Yield: approximately 30

Cocktail Olive Balls

1   stick butter, softened
1   cup flour
1   (5 ounce) small glass jar Old
    English cheese
1   bottle stuffed olives (any
    flavor)

Mix butter, flour and cheese to form the dough mixture. Make into balls, wrapping each around an olive. Bake at 300 degrees for 10-15 minutes. May be made ahead and frozen.

Mustard Pickles

2   quarts small white onions, scalded and peeled
2   quarts cucumbers, unpeeled and sliced (can be half small pickling cucumbers and half large cucumbers)
2   big heads cauliflower
3   red peppers, seeded and chopped
2   green peppers, seeded and chopped
1   bunch celery
1   cup salt

SAUCE:

3¹/₄ quarts white vinegar
1   quart water
2   tablespoons turmeric
2¹/₂ cups sugar
10 tablespoons dry mustard
2   cups all-purpose flour
2   tablespoons celery seed
2   tablespoons mustard seed

In a large bowl combine vegetables and cover with brine made of 1 gallon water and 1 cup salt and let stand 24 hours. Then scald but don't boil. Drain.

In saucepan combine white vinegar, water, turmeric, sugar, dry mustard and flour. Heat over medium heat stirring constantly until thick. Put drained vegetables in and reheat to the boiling point but DO NOT boil. Add mustard and celery seeds. Immediately pour mixture into heated bottles while very hot, leaving a ¹/₂-inch headspace. Screw on lids and wait for them to seal. Wait 2 weeks to eat.

Yield: 15-16 pints

Note: Increase the amount of sauce if you find that you run dry at the end of the bottling process.

Also known as "Pustard Mickels." Description featured on page 3.

Rum Slush

26 ounces light rum
3   (6 ounce) cans frozen limeade concentrate
6   (12 ounce) cans 7-up®

Combine all ingredients in a 1 gallon tub. Place in freezer for 24 hours. Can be re-frozen.

Frozen Spiked Tea

7   cups water
1   cup sugar
4   tea bags, orange spice is best
1   (12 ounce) can orange juice
    concentrate, thawed
1   (12 ounce) can lemonade
    concentrate, thawed
1   cup vodka
Sprite® or club soda

Boil water and sugar until sugar dissolves. Remove from heat. Add tea bags and let steep until cool. Stir in remaining ingredients. Pour into large plastic container with cover. Cover and freeze at least 8 hours. To serve: Scoop out partially frozen mixture and add Sprite® or club soda into a slush consistency.

Yield: 10-12 servings

Holiday Punch

32   ounce cranberry cocktail
46   ounces unsweetened pineapple
     juice
2   cups orange juice
$^2/_3$ cup lemon juice
$^1/_2$ cup sugar
33   ounces ginger ale
vodka to taste

Combine all ingredients and keep chilled.

Garnish with cranberries.

Citric Punch

2   cups hot water
6   cups sugar
1   (46 ounce) can pineapple juice
1   (12 ounce) can frozen orange
    juice
1   (6 ounce) can frozen lemon
    juice (not lemonade)
1   tablespoon vanilla
1   tablespoon almond extract
2   gallons water
$^1/_3$ cup citric acid (purchase at
    pharmacy)

Dissolve 6 cups sugar in 2 cups hot water. Dissolve $^1/_3$ cup citric acid in $^1/_2$ cup hot water.

Combine with all remaining ingredients and keep chilled.

Yield: 3 gallons

Notes:

Mid-day Masterpieces
BRUNCH & BREADS

Painting by: Scott Wallis

I n the early days, Ogden's reputation as a wide-open western town with a wide variety of unsavory activities spread throughout the West. In addition to saloons and even opium dens, a red light district was prevalent in the area of 25th Street for eight decades - from the coming of the railroad through the era of World War II. Known as "Two-Bit" Street in its hey day, 25th Street is anchored by Union Station to the west with legends of underground tunnels that stretched beneath the downtown area. Today, the notoriously charming historic street offers an eclectic mix of shopping, dining and nightlife.

Paintings by: Cara Koolmees

Originally housing everything from Chinese laundries to houses of ill repute in the early 1900's, Ogden's Historic 25th Street is a fun place to explore any time of the year. The restored buildings now feature quaint shops, tasteful restaurants and trendy clubs and pubs.

BRUNCH & BREADS

Oven Omelet

2   cups Cheddar cheese,
     shredded
1   (4 ounce) can green chilies,
     drained and chopped
2   cups Monterey Jack cheese,
     shredded
1¼ cups milk
3   tablespoons flour
½   teaspoon salt
3   eggs
1   (8 ounce) can tomato sauce

Layer Cheddar cheese, chilies and Monterey Jack cheese in 8x8-inch greased pan. Repeat layers starting with Cheddar cheese. Beat milk, flour, salt and eggs: pour over cheese/chili mixture. Bake uncovered at 350 degrees until set in center and top is golden brown, approximately 40 minutes. Remove and let stand for 10 minutes before cutting. Heat tomato sauce and serve with omelet.

Serves: 8

Sunday Brunch Casserole

½   pound sausage
1   pound bacon
½   cup onion, chopped
½   cup green pepper, chopped
12 eggs
1   cup milk
1   (16 ounce) package frozen
     hash browns, thawed
1   cup Cheddar cheese, shredded
1   teaspoon salt
½   teaspoon pepper
¼   teaspoon dill

In a skillet, cook bacon and sausage, reserve drippings. Crumble bacon and set aside. Sauté onions and green peppers in drippings until tender. In large bowl beat eggs and milk. Stir in hash browns, salt, pepper, dill, onion, cheese, green pepper and meat. Place in a greased 9x13-inch baking dish. Bake uncovered at 350 degrees for 40-45 minutes.

Servings: 8-10

Triple Cheese Bake

5 cups soft bread cubes

3 tablespoons butter, melted

1½ cups Swiss cheese, shredded

¼ cup Monterey Jack cheese, shredded

1 pound bacon, cooked, drained and crumbled

8 eggs

1⅔ cups milk

¼ cup white wine

2 whole green onions, minced

1 tablespoon brown mustard

½ cup sour cream

½ cup Parmesan cheese, grated

Spread bread cubes on bottom of greased 9x13-inch pan. Drizzle butter over bread. Sprinkle with Swiss and Jack cheeses. Add bacon. Whisk together eggs, milk, wine, onions and mustard. Pour over mixture in baking dish. Cover with foil and refrigerate at least 6 hours. Let sit at room temperature for 30 minutes before baking. Cover and bake at 325 degrees for 1 hour, or until set. Combine sour cream and Parmesan cheese. Spread over baked mixture. Return to oven uncovered, cook until crusty and lightly browned, about 10 minutes.

Servings: 8

Vegetable Frittata with Asiago Cheese

1½ teaspoons olive oil

1 medium-sized red onion, chopped

1 red bell pepper, coarsely chopped

1 medium zucchini, chopped

2 cups (packed) spinach leaves, torn into 1-inch pieces

3 large eggs

6 large egg whites

½ teaspoon salt

¼ teaspoon ground black pepper

1 ounce Asiago cheese, shaved

1 cup tomatoes, chopped

1 tablespoons fresh basil, chopped

Preheat broiler. Heat olive oil in 10-inch non-stick oven-proof skillet over medium high heat. Add onion and bell pepper; sauté until golden, about 8 minutes. Add zucchini; sauté until tender, about 5 minutes. Add spinach; stir until wilted, about 1 minute. Season with salt and pepper.

Whisk eggs, egg whites, salt and pepper in medium bowl to blend. Pour egg mixture over hot vegetables in skillet; stir gently to combine. Reduce heat to medium-low. Cook without stirring until eggs are set on bottom, about 5 minutes.

Sprinkle cheese over frittata. Broil until cheese melts, about 2 minutes. Top with tomatoes and basil.

Servings: 4-6

Chili Relleno Casserole

CASSEROLE:

4 eggs

1 1/2 cups milk

2 tablespoons flour

1/2 teaspoon pepper

1/4 teaspoon salt

dash of oregano

dash of chili powder

3 (7 ounce) cans whole green chilies, split open (reserve liquid)

4 cups Cheddar cheese, shredded (approximately 1 pound)

4 cups Monterey Jack cheese, shredded (approximately 1 pound)

SAUCE:

1 (8 ounce) can tomatoes

1 medium onion

1 clove garlic

oregano

salt and pepper

1 (14.5 ounce) can chicken broth

liquid from chilies (approximately 2 cups)

oil

To make casserole: Preheat oven to 350 degrees. Lightly grease a 9x13-inch glass baking dish. Beat eggs, milk, flour, pepper, salt, oregano and chili powder in a medium bowl. Arrange 1/3 of chilies in prepared dish, covering completely. Sprinkle with 1/3 of each cheese. Repeat layering twice. Pour egg mixture over cheese. Let stand 30 minutes, cover and refrigerate (can be prepared 1 day ahead). Bake uncovered until casserole is slightly puffed in center and golden brown on edges, about 45 minutes. Cool 20 minutes and serve with accompanying sauce.

To make sauce: Sauté onion and garlic in oil. Add tomatoes, liquid and spices. Reduce heat and simmer 3 hours, then pureé.

Dining Car Special
CARROT BREAD

4 eggs

2 cups sugar

1 1/2 cups vegetable oil

3 cups flour

2 teaspoons baking powder

1 1/2 teaspoons baking soda

1/4 teaspoon salt

2 teaspoons cinnamon

2 cups raw carrots, finely shredded

Optional: raisins or chopped nuts

In a mixing bowl beat eggs. Add sugar and beat until thick. Add oil gradually, beating until well-blended. Stir in flour, baking powder, baking soda, salt and cinnamon. Mix until smooth. Stir in carrots. Add raisins or nuts if desired. Pour batter into 2 well-greased bread tins. Bake at 350 degrees for 1 hour.

Yield: 2 Loaves

Goat Cheese, Artichoke & Smoked Ham Strata

2 cups whole milk

¼ cup olive oil

8 cups 1-inch cubes sourdough bread, crusts trimmed

1½ cups whipping cream

5 large eggs

1 tablespoon garlic, chopped

1½ teaspoons salt

¾ teaspoon black pepper

½ teaspoon ground nutmeg

12 ounces soft fresh goat cheese (such as Montrachet), crumbled (about 3 cups)

2 tablespoons fresh sage, chopped

1 tablespoon fresh thyme, chopped

1½ teaspoons dried basil

12 ounces smoked ham, chopped

3 (6½ ounce) jars marinated artichoke hearts, drained, halved lengthwise, about 2¼ cups

1 cup (packed) fontina cheese, grated

1½ cups (packed) Parmesan cheese, grated

Preheat oven to 350 degrees. Butter 9x13-inch glass baking dish. Whisk milk and oil in large bowl. Stir in bread. Let stand until liquid is absorbed, about 10 minutes.

Whisk cream and next 5 ingredients in another large bowl to blend. Add goat cheese. Mix herbs in small bowl to blend.

Place half of bread mixture in prepared dish. Top with half of ham, artichoke hearts, herbs and cheeses. Pour half of cream mixture over. Repeat layering with remaining bread, ham, artichoke hearts, herbs, cheeses and cream mixture. (Can be made 1 day ahead.) Cover and chill.

Bake uncovered until firm in center and brown around edges, about 1 hour.

Servings: 8

Pastry Dough

1¼ cups all-purpose flour

¾ stick (6 tablespoons) cold unsalted butter, cut into bits

2 tablespoons cold vegetable shortening

¼ teaspoon salt

2-4 tablespoons ice water

In a bowl with a pastry blender or in a food processor blend or pulse together flour, butter, shortening and salt until mixture resembles coarse meal. Add 2 tablespoons ice water and toss or pulse until incorporated. Add enough remaining ice water, 1 tablespoon at a time, tossing with a fork or pulsing to incorporate, to begin to form a dough.

On a work surface knead dough in 3 or 4 forward motions with heel of hand to make dough easier to work with. Form dough into a ball and flatten to form a disk. Wrap dough in plastic wrap and chill 1 hour.

Makes enough dough for a single-crust 9-10-inch pie or an 11-inch tart.

Herbed Goat Cheese Tart

pastry dough (above)

10 ounces soft mild goat cheese

1 cup cottage cheese

3 large egg yolks

¼ cup all-purpose flour

1 stick (½ cup) unsalted butter, softened

1 tablespoon mixed fresh herbs such as thyme, rosemary and lavender, chopped

2-3 tablespoons mixed whole fresh herb leaves

On a lightly floured surface with a floured rolling pin roll out dough into a 13-inch round (about ⅛-inch thick) and fit into a 10-11-inch round tart pan with a removable rim. Prick dough all over with a fork and chill 30 minutes.

Preheat oven to 350 degrees. Bake tart shell on a baking sheet in middle of oven 10 minutes, or until almost cooked through but still pale.

In a food processor blend cheeses, yolks, flour and butter until smooth. Stir in chopped herbs and pour filling into tart shell. Bake tart 20 minutes, or until filling is just set. Sprinkle tart with herb leaves and continue baking until filling and crust are pale golden. Cool tart in pan on a rack and remove rim. Serve tart warm or at room temperature.

Servings: 6-8

Baja Bites

10 eggs
2   cups cottage cheese
1/2 cup flour
1   teaspoon baking powder
1/2 cup butter, melted
4   tablespoons green onion, minced
2   (4 ounce) cans green chilies, chopped
4   cups Monterey Jack cheese, shredded

Beat eggs until well blended. Add cottage cheese and blend. Combine flour and baking powder; add to egg mixture. Add melted butter; stir in green onion, chilies and cheese. Pour into greased 9x13-inch baking pan. Sprinkle more cheese on top. Bake at 350 degrees for 45-50 minutes, until firm in center. Let set before cutting.

Servings: 8-10

Ogden Oven Popovers

1/4-1/2 cup butter
1 1/2 cups milk
6   eggs
1   teaspoon vanilla
1 1/2 cups flour

Melt butter in oven while preheating to 425 degrees in a large deep dish (9x13-inch or bigger). When butter is melted, remove pan from oven. In blender, combine milk, eggs, vanilla and flour. Blend for 3-5 minutes. Pour on top of melted butter. Bake at 425 degrees for 12 minutes. Reduce heat to 300 degrees and bake an additional 12 minutes.

Serve with fresh fruit, powdered sugar or sour cream and strawberries.

Banana Blueberry Muffins

1   stick butter, softened
3/4 cup white sugar
2   eggs
3   bananas, mashed
1/2 cup milk
2   cups flour
2   teaspoons baking powder
1/2 teaspoon ground cinnamon
2   cups fresh blueberries

Mix ingredients in order, carefully stirring in the blueberries. Spoon the batter into greased muffin tins filling cups to the top. Bake at 375 degrees for 30-35 minutes.

Yield: 1 dozen

Crustless Quiche

6   eggs, beaten
2   tablespoons heavy cream
1   can cream of celery soup
1   cup Cheddar cheese
1   cup provolone cheese
1   teaspoon seasoned salt
2   cups filling of choice
     (see suggestions)

Prepare quiche by combining eggs, cream of celery soup, cheeses and salt. Add filling ingredients of your choice. Great favorites are: garden vegetable with spinach, feta and colorful peppers, shrimp, fresh dill and asparagus or artichokes, ham, mushrooms and asparagus, fresh corn and bacon. Be creative with herbs and spices.

Spray 10-inch pie plate with non-stick cooking spray and bake 1 hour at 350 degrees or until set. Cool 10 minutes before cutting. May also bake in mini muffin tins, sprayed with non-stick cooking spray, for 15-20 minutes.

Serve these for afternoon tea or appetizer.

RESTAURANT FEATURE

The Greenery's Mormon Muffin

2   cups water, boiling
5   teaspoons baking soda
1   cup shortening
2   cups sugar
4   eggs
1   quart buttermilk
5   cups flour
1   teaspoon salt
4   cups All-Bran® cereal
2   cups bran flakes
1   cup walnuts, chopped

Add baking soda to boiling water and set aside. Whip shortening and sugar until light and fluffy. Add the eggs slowly. Mix well. Add buttermilk, flour, salt and mix well. Add soda water very slowly. Gently fold cereals and nuts into the mix. Let muffin mix sit in the refrigerator overnight before baking. (Muffin mix will last one week, covered and refrigerated.) Stir batter. Spoon $1/8$ cup into each greased muffin tin. Bake at 350 degrees for 20-30 minutes. Cool 5 minutes.

Servings: 3 dozen

Located at the Mouth of Ogden Canyon, The Greenery boasts scenic views of the Wasatch Mountains. Crowds once flocked to this historic spot for its natural hot springs. Today's fine gifts and unique eatery still attract visitors and locals.

Tomato-Rosemary Biscuits

1³/₄ cups flour

¹/₃ cup Parmesan cheese, grated

2 tablespoons sugar

2 teaspoons baking powder

¹/₂ teaspoon dried rosemary, crushed

¹/₄ teaspoon baking soda

¹/₈ teaspoon garlic powder

¹/₈ teaspoon pepper

1 beaten egg

¹/₂ cup milk

¹/₂ cup tomato sauce

¹/₃ cup olive oil

Parmesan cheese, grated

In a bowl, stir together flour, Parmesan cheese, sugar, baking powder, rosemary, baking soda, garlic powder and pepper. Make a well in center. Combine egg, milk, tomato sauce and oil. Add all at once to flour mixture. Stir just until moistened (the batter should be lumpy). Lightly grease a regular-size muffin tin. Fill each cup ²/₃ full. If desired, sprinkle the tops with additional Parmesan cheese. Bake at 350 degrees for 20-24 minutes, or until light brown. Remove from pan and cool on a wire rack. Best when served warm.

Servings: 12 biscuits

Dining Car Special
PERFECT ORANGE ROLLS

2 packages active dry yeast

¹/₄ cup warm water

1¹/₄ cup milk, scalded

¹/₂ teaspoon salt

¹/₂ cup sugar

¹/₂ cup margarine or butter

3 eggs, well beaten

5-5¹/₂ cups flour

ORANGE-SUGAR MIXTURE

1 cup sugar

¹/₂ cup butter

grated zest from 2 oranges

Dissolve yeast in warm water and set aside. Scald milk; add sugar, butter and salt; stir to dissolve sugar. Cool mixture to lukewarm and add to yeast. Beat eggs until light and fluffy. Beat them into yeast mixture. Add 2 cups of flour and beat with mixer. Add rest of flour, blending it by hand. Knead it for 5 minutes. Cover dough and allow to rise until double in bulk. Divide dough in half. Roll it out into a rectangle 18-inches long and ¹/₄-inch thick. Cream together the sugar, butter and orange zest and spread it over the dough. Roll it up jelly roll style. Cut the dough into 1-inch slices. Place in greased muffin pans. Let it rise until double in bulk. Dough can be refrigerated 1 day in advance. Allow to reach room temperature approximately 3 hours before making rolls. Bake 12-15 minutes at 375 degrees.

Yield: 3 dozen

Blue Cheese Biscuits

1   package refrigerator dough
       biscuits (10-12)
4   tablespoons blue cheese,
       crumbled
$^{1}/_{2}$ cup butter

Preheat oven to 375 degrees. Cut biscuits into quarters and place equal amounts in each tin of a 12-cup muffin tin. Melt together the butter and blue cheese; pour mixture over biscuits. Bake 10-15 minutes or until golden brown. Serve hot.

Beer Bread

$^{1}/_{4}$-$^{1}/_{2}$ cup butter, melted
3   cups self-rising flour
2   tablespoons sugar
1   (12 ounce) can beer

Pour enough melted butter into a 9x5-inch pan to coat the bottom. In a bowl, mix remaining ingredients together. Spoon dough into loaf pan. Pour remaining butter on top. Bake at 350 degrees for 50-60 minutes until bread is light gold in color. Let stand 15 minutes before cutting. Serve warm.

Yield: 1 loaf

Pumpkin Bread

5   cups all-purpose flour
3   teaspoons baking soda
$2^{1}/_{4}$ teaspoons salt
1   tablespoon + $1^{1}/_{2}$ teaspoons
       ground cinnamon
1   tablespoon + $1^{1}/_{2}$ teaspoons
       ground nutmeg
$^{1}/_{2}$ teaspoon ground ginger
$4^{1}/_{2}$ cups sugar
$1^{1}/_{2}$ cups vegetable oil
6   eggs
1   cup cold water
1   (29 ounce) can pumpkin

Sift flour, baking soda, salt, cinnamon, nutmeg, ginger and sugar into a large bowl and mix well. Add oil, eggs, water and pumpkin. Beat until smooth. Pour batter into 2 large or 4 small loaf pans. Bake at 350 degrees for 50-60 minutes.

Yield: 2 large or 4 small loaves

Sugared Bacon

1 pound bacon
1 cup brown sugar

Lay sliced bacon on jelly-roll pan. Let come to room temperature (30 minutes). Paste each slice heavily with brown sugar. Bake in 350 degrees oven until done. Remove from pan and place on brown paper to cool.

Mom's Buttermilk Pancakes

3³/₄ cups all-purpose flour
¹/₄ cup sugar
3 teaspoons baking soda
³/₄ teaspoon salt
4 eggs, beaten
1 quart buttermilk
¹/₄ cup oil

In a mixing bowl stir together flour, sugar, baking soda and salt. In another mixing bowl combine eggs, buttermilk and oil. Add to flour mixture all at once. Stir mixture just until blended but still slightly lumpy. Keeps 2-3 days in refrigerator.

Pour about ¹/₄ cup batter onto a hot, lightly greased griddle or heavy skillet for each standard-size pancake. Cook until pancakes are golden brown, turning to cook second sides when pancakes have bubbly surfaces and slightly dry edges.

Yield: 24-30 standard-size cakes

Banana Bread

¹/₃ cup butter, softened
1 cup sugar
2 eggs
3 tablespoons sour milk (add a drop of vinegar to warm milk)
1 teaspoon baking soda
1 teaspoon baking powder
¹/₂ teaspoon salt
2 cups flour
3 bananas, mashed

Mix together all ingredients in order given. Bake in a large greased bread pan at 350 degrees for 1 hour or until tester comes out clean.

Servings: 1 loaf

Spinach-Filled Crepes

CREPE BATTER:

1   cup milk

$^3/_4$ cup unsifted all-purpose flour

1   teaspoon sugar

$^1/_2$ teaspoon salt

2   tablespoons vegetable oil

4   eggs

vegetable oil

CHEESE SAUCE:

$^1/_3$ cup butter or margarine

$^1/_3$ cup unsifted all-purpose flour

1   teaspoon salt

$^1/_8$ teaspoon pepper

$^1/_2$ teaspoon dry mustard

$2^1/_2$ cups milk

$1^1/_2$ cups (6 ounces) sharp
      Cheddar cheese, grated

FILLING:

2   (10 ounce)packages frozen
      chopped spinach, thawed and
      drained

6   tablespoons butter or
      margarine

$^1/_2$ pound mushrooms, washed
      coarsely chopped (2 cups)

GARNISH:

1   whole mushroom, sliced

1   tablespoon fresh parsley,
      chopped

Day before, make batter: With rotary beater, beat milk, flour, sugar, salt and oil. Add eggs; beat until blended. Refrigerate, covered, overnight.

Next day, make crepes: Slowly heat 8-inch skillet over medium heat just until a drop of water sizzles. Brush pan lightly with vegetable oil. Pour $^1/_4$ cup batter into skillet, tilting pan so batter covers bottom completely. Cook until top is dry and bottom lightly browned; with spatula, turn and brown other side. Remove to wire rack and cool; stack between squares of waxed paper. Repeat with rest of batter; brush pan with oil each time. Yields 10.

To make cheese sauce: Heat butter just until melted; remove from heat. Add flour, salt, pepper and mustard. Stir until smooth. Add milk slowly, stirring constantly. Return to heat. Over medium heat bring sauce to boil, stirring constantly. Add cheese; stirring over low heat just until melted. Remove from heat. Yields 3 cups.

To make filling: Drain spinach well. In a 10-inch skillet, use butter to sauté spinach and mushrooms, about 2 minutes. Remove from heat. Reserve $^1/_2$ cup cheese sauce. Combine rest of sauce with spinach-mushroom mixture and mix well. Preheat oven to 350 degrees. Assemble crepes on buttered, heat-proof serving dish or cookie sheet. Place a crepe on dish. Spread with $^1/_4$ cup filling. Top with another crepe. Continue stacking crepes and filling. End with plain crepe on top. Cover completely with foil; heat in oven 20 minutes.

Remove foil. Spoon reserved cheese sauce over top. Garnish with sliced mushrooms and parsley. Cut into wedges.

Servings: 8

Scottish Scones

SCONES:

1½ cups all-purpose or
     unbleached flour

¾ cup rolled oats

¼ cup brown sugar, firmly
     packed

2   teaspoons baking powder

½ teaspoon salt

½ teaspoon cinnamon

½ cup margarine or butter

½ cup milk

TOPPING:

1   tablespoon margarine or
     butter, melted

1   tablespoon sugar

¼ teaspoon cinnamon

Heat oven to 375 degrees. Lightly grease cookie sheet. Spoon flour into measuring cup; level off. In medium bowl, combine flour, oats, brown sugar, baking powder, salt and cinnamon; blend well. Using pastry blender or fork, cut in margarine until mixture is crumbly. Add milk all at once stirring just until moistened. On floured surface, knead dough gently 5 or 6 times. Press into 6-inch circle, about 1-inch thick; place on prepared cookie sheet. Brush top with melted margarine. Combine sugar and cinnamon; sprinkle over top. Cut into 8 wedges; separate slightly. Bake at 375 degrees for 20-30 minutes or until golden brown. Serve warm.

Yield: 8 scones

French Doughnuts

MUFFINS:

5   tablespoons butter, softened

½ cup sugar

1   egg beaten

1½ cups flour

2¼ teaspoon baking powder

¼ teaspoon salt

¼ teaspoon nutmeg

½ cup milk

TOPPING:

⅓ butter, melted

⅓ cup sugar

½ teaspoon cinnamon

To make muffins: Cream together butter and sugar. Add egg and mix well. Sift dry ingredients together. Add dry mixture alternately with milk. Pour into greased muffin tins. Bake at 350 degrees for 25-30 minutes.

To make topping: Remove from pans; roll in melted butter and then in a mixture of sugar and cinnamon.

Yield: 12 muffins

Orange Scones with Berries & Cream

2 cups sifted all-purpose flour

1 tablespoon baking powder

1 teaspoon salt

2 tablespoons granulated sugar

5$^1/_2$ tablespoons unsalted butter

1 extra large egg, beaten

$^1/_2$ cup whipping cream

2 tablespoons unsalted butter, melted

$^1/_2$ cup granulated sugar

1 tablespoon orange zest

6-8 cups fresh berries, washed and dried

$^3/_4$-1 cup granulated sugar, depending upon berry sweetness

1-1$^1/_2$ cups whipping cream, whipped and lightly sweetened with 2 tablespoons powdered sugar

Preheat the oven to 425 degrees. In a small bowl, stir together the flour, baking powder, salt and sugar. Cut in the butter using a pastry blender or 2 knives. In a small bowl, combine the beaten egg and cream. Add to the flour mixture. Mix until just blended. Turn out batter onto a lightly floured board and knead for 1 minute. Roll dough into a rectangle approximately 4x8-inches. Brush dough with melted butter. Sprinkle with sugar and orange zest. Roll up, jelly roll fashion and seal the long seam by pinching it together lightly with your fingers. Cut roll into 8 1-inch thick slices. Lay slices down sideways (cut side down) on a lightly greased baking sheet and bake for 12-15 minutes, or until scones are golden.

Place berries in a large bowl. Sprinkle with sugar and refrigerate for 1-2 hours. To serve, spoon berries over scones and top with freshly whipped cream.

Yield: 8 scones

Notes:

Painting by: Blanche P. Wilson

From easy trail walks to canyon-rim hikes, Ogden's pathways offer unparalleled scenic beauty. The Ogden River Parkway stretches for more than three miles, offering walking, biking, picnicking and fishing within the city limits. Downtown Ogden features a Gold Medal mile, an Olympic Legacy of the 2002 Winter Olympics, to encourage fitness. This urban pathway leads visitors past a series of life-sized bronze statues of children reminiscent of Ogden City's colorful history. Hiking trails are also scattered throughout the Wasatch and Cache National Forests. Trails include the Indian Trail, a five-mile hike beginning near the base of Ogden Canyon; the Skyline Trailhead, a nine-mile trek to the 9,712 foot summit of Ben Lomond Peak; and the Pineview Trailhead, a 22-mile hike.

Painting by: Shanna Kunz

SOUPS & SALADS

Cream of Mushroom Soup

5	cups water
5	chicken bouillon cubes
1	pound fresh mushrooms, sliced
$^1/_2$	cup butter
5	tablespoons flour
1	cup cream or half-and-half

Dissolve chicken bouillon cubes in water to make broth.

Sauté mushrooms in butter. Add flour. Gradually stir in broth; simmer. Remove from heat; add cream or half-and-half.

Return to heat but do not boil.

Cream of Brie Soup

$^1/_2$	cup onions, finely chopped
$^1/_2$	cup celery, finely chopped
4	tablespoons butter
$^1/_4$	cup flour
2	cups half-and-half
2	cups chicken broth
$^3/_4$	pound brie cheese, rind removed, cubed

In an 8-quart pot, sauté onion and celery in butter. Do not brown. Stir in flour. Remove from heat and stir in half-and-half and chicken broth.

Return to heat and stir until soup thickens. Do not boil.

Add cheese to pot. Stir until melted. Serve immediately.

Leek and Stilton Soup with Port

1 cup leek (white and pale green part of leek), finely chopped
1 large garlic clove, minced
1/2 cup celery, finely chopped
1/2 cup carrot, finely chopped
1 bay leaf
1/2 teaspoon dried thyme, crumbled
2 tablespoons unsalted butter
2 russet (baking) potatoes (about 1 pound), peeled and thinly sliced
3 cups chicken broth
1 cup half-and-half
6 ounces Stilton cheese, crumbled (about 1 1/2 cups)
3 tablespoons tawny port or to taste
fresh chives, minced for garnish

In a large saucepan cook the leek, garlic, celery and carrot with the bay leaf and thyme in the butter over moderate heat, stirring, for 5 minutes or until the vegetables are softened.

Add the potatoes and broth and simmer, covered for 15 minutes or until potatoes are very tender.

Discard bay leaf and purée the soup in batches in the blender. Transfer the puree to a clean pan and stir in the half-and-half.

Heat the soup over low heat, whisk in the Stilton, whisking until the cheese is melted and the soup is smooth. Whisk in port and salt and pepper to taste. Do not let soup boil.

Garnish with chives.

Servings: 6

Cheddar Soup

1 large onion, minced
1 stalk celery, minced
2 tablespoons melted butter
1 tablespoon flour
1 teaspoon ground dried mustard
1 teaspoon paprika
3 cups chicken broth
2 cups half-and-half
2 cups Cheddar cheese, grated
minced dill to garnish
salt to taste

Sauté onion and celery gently in butter until transparent, about 8 minutes. Stir in flour and cook until mixture bubbles. Stir in mustard and paprika. Slowly add broth, bring to a boil, simmer for 10 minutes. Stir in half-and-half. Add cheese a little at a time, stirring constantly until cheese is melted. Do not boil. Add salt to taste.

Garnish with minced dill.

Best Ever Minestrone Soup

2   cups ground beef, cooked and drained

1   (28 ounce) can tomatoes, puréed

1   quart water

2   large carrots, peeled and sliced

2   (8 ounce) cans tomato sauce

2   cups beef broth

1   tablespoon dried parsley leaves

$^1/_2$ teaspoon basil leaves

1   teaspoon dried oregano leaves

$^1/_2$ teaspoon pepper

$^1/_2$ teaspoon garlic salt

1   (15 ounce) can garbanzo beans, drained

1   (16 ounce) can green beans, drained

1   (15 ounce) can kidney beans, drained

$1^1/_2$ cups mostaccioli pasta, uncooked

In large dutch oven, combine meat, tomatoes, water, carrots, tomato sauce, broth, parsley, basil, oregano, pepper and garlic salt. Bring to a boil, simmer on low heat for 20 minutes. Add garbanzo, green and kidney beans. Bring to a boil. Add pasta. Simmer 10-12 minutes until tender. Season to taste.

Servings: 10-12

Painting by: Scott Wallis

Sweet Pepper & Roasted Tomato Soup with Focaccia Croutons

2 pounds vine-ripe tomatoes, cut into quarters

2 teaspoons garlic, chopped

1 teaspoon kosher salt

$^1/_8$ teaspoon pepper

2 tablespoons balsamic vinegar

2 tablespoons extra virgin olive oil

1 (6 ounce) jar sweet pepper pesto

1 cup focaccia croutons

$^1/_2$ cup golden yellow tomatoes, chopped

2 tablespoons fresh basil leaves, cut into julienne

2 tablespoons Mediterranean tangerine oil

In ovenproof dish, add tomatoes, vinegar, olive oil, garlic, salt and pepper. Roast in 350 degree oven for 30-40 minutes or until tomatoes are bubbly and flesh is soft. Pureé in blender and strain or pass through a food mill. Add pesto. Divide soup into 4 bowls and top with croutons, chopped tomato and fresh basil. Drizzle with tangerine oil.

To make focaccia croutons: Cut focaccia bread (found in specialty bakeries) into 1-inch cubes. Toast in 350 degrees oven until browned.

Farmers' Market Vegetable Soup

$^2/_3$ cup carrot, sliced

$^1/_2$ cup onion, diced

2 garlic cloves, minced

2 tablespoons olive oil

3 cups broth (beef, chicken, vegetable)

$1^1/_2$ cups green cabbage, diced

$^1/_2$ cup green beans, diced

1 tablespoon tomato paste

$^1/_2$ teaspoon dried basil

$^1/_4$ teaspoon dried oregano

$^1/_3$ teaspoon salt

$^1/_2$ cup zucchini, diced

Sauté the carrot, onion and garlic in olive oil over low heat until softened (about 5 minutes). Add broth, cabbage, beans, tomato paste, basil, oregano and salt. Bring to a boil.

Lower the heat and simmer, covered, about 15 minutes or until the beans are tender. Stir in zucchini and heat 3-4 minutes. Serve hot.

Servings: 4

Dining Car Special
COLD SHRIMP SOUP

1 quart tomato juice

1 (8 ounce) bottle shrimp sauce

2 small cans shrimp

2 cups diced celery

$^1/_2$ cup diced green pepper

$^1/_2$ cup sugar (scant)

2 tablespoons lemon juice

1 tablespoon Worcestershire sauce

$1^1/_2$ teaspoon horseradish

$^1/_2$ teaspoon garlic salt

1 minced onion

salt to taste

Combine all ingredients and chill overnight.

Servings: 6-8

Hamburger Wild Rice Soup

1   pound ground beef
2   cups cooked wild rice, about
    $^1/_2$ cup uncooked
1   ($10^1/_2$ ounce) can cream of
    potato soup
1   ($10^1/_2$ ounce) can cream of
    asparagus soup or cream of
    celery soup
2   cups canned milk
1   cup Cheddar cheese, shredded
1   teaspoon garlic salt
1   teaspoon dried parsley flakes

Brown the ground beef and drain. Prepare wild rice according to package directions.

Combine the soups, milk and cheese and blend. Add wild rice and ground beef and simmer until cheese has melted.

Add garlic and parsley, adjusting seasonings to taste.

Servings: 4-6

RESTAURANT FEATURE

Sandy's Ham & Lima Bean Soup

4   cups dry lima beans
$^1/_4$ tablespoon white pepper
1   teaspoon parsley, minced
1   small onion, diced
1   head celery, diced (leaves
      included)
$^1/_2$ cup carrots, shredded
$^1/_4$ cup ham base paste or ham
      hocks
2   cups ham, diced
2   tablespoons butter, cubed

Pour lima beans in a large stock pot. Add celery, onion and carrots. Stir in 1 gallon of water and add ham base paste. Sprinkle white pepper and parsley on top of the water and add butter. Bring to a boil and continue for 30 minutes (will boil down). Begin checking beans for desired tenderness. Continue cooking until beans are tender. Reduce heat and add ham.

Stir and serve.

Sandy's Fine Foods, offers down home good cookin'.
Family owned and operated in Ogden since 1976.

Tomato Soup

2¼ sticks of butter

3 tablespoons olive oil

1½ large onion, sliced

¾ teaspoon thyme

¾ teaspoon basil

3¾ pounds fresh tomatoes, peeled or 1 large (28 ounce) can Italian tomatoes

4½ tablespoons tomato paste

⅓ cup flour

5½ cups chicken broth

2 teaspoons sugar

1½ cups cream or half-and-half

salt and pepper to taste

Combine 2 sticks butter and olive oil in 6-quart pot. Add onion, thyme, basil, salt and pepper. Cook until tender. Add tomatoes and tomato paste. Blend flour into ½ cup chicken broth and stir into tomato mixture. Add remaining 5 cups chicken broth and simmer 30 minutes. Transfer soup to food processor and purée. (Mixture can be frozen at this point for later use. When ready to serve, defrost and continue recipe as follows.)

Heat sugar and cream. Simmer 5 minutes. Add ¼ stick butter. Add tomato mixture. Stir thoroughly.

May be served hot or cold.

Servings: 9-12

Thai Style Carrot Soup

1 tablespoon butter

1 tablespoon canola oil

2 leeks, cleaned and sliced

1 stalk lemon grass, minced

1 (¾-inch) piece of ginger, grated

½ teaspoon green Thai curry paste

6 large carrots, peeled and coarsely sliced

½ can coconut milk

1 quart chicken stock

salt and pepper to taste

GARNISH:

plain yogurt

fresh cilantro

Heat butter and oil over medium heat. Sauté leeks until soft and wilted. Add lemon grass, ginger and curry paste. Cook until fragrant. Add carrots, stir to coat. Add stock and cook until carrots are soft. Remove from heat, add coconut milk. Then pureé in blender or food processor.

Garnish with yogurt and/or cilantro.

Serves: 5-6

Snow Chili

½ onion

2 garlic cloves, chopped

1 tablespoon olive oil

½ teaspoon red pepper

1 teaspoon cumin

½ teaspoon black pepper

3 cans white beans, undrained

2 cans white corn, undrained

4 cubes chicken bouillon

1 (4 ounce) can chopped green chilies

1 boiled chicken breast, cut into small pieces

Sauté onion and garlic in oil over low heat until softened, about 2 minutes, in an 8 quart saucepan. Add red pepper, cumin and black pepper to mixture, stir.

Add beans, corn, bouillon, chilies and chicken to mixture. Continue cooking on medium heat about 15 minutes or until the beans are tender.

Veal Stew

1 pound veal stew meat, cut up

olive oil and butter

¼ cup white wine

1 (14 ½ ounce) can beef broth

½ package frozen small green peas with pearl onions

cornstarch

In a cast iron frying pan, brown small batches of meat in olive oil and butter. Remove meat and deglaze pan with white wine, scraping brown bits from the bottom of the pan.

Return meat to pan, adding some beef broth and simmering for about an hour and a half or until the meat is tender. Add beef broth as needed to prevent sticking and burning.

About 5 minutes before serving, add frozen peas. Broth may be thickened to desired consistency by adding cornstarch with water to desired thickness.

Serve over rice, etc.

Roosters' Turkey Chili

³/₄ cup water

¹/₂ cup flour

2 cups onion, chopped

2 cups celery, chopped

1 (28 ounce) can whole tomatoes, puréed

1 (28 ounce) can tomatoes, diced

6 (6 ounce) cans green chilies, puréed

6 cups turkey stock (if available) or chicken broth

6 chicken bouillon cubes

¹/₄ cup chili powder

1 teaspoon ground cumin

1 tablespoon ground oregano

1 tablespoon hot sauce of choice

2 pounds cooked turkey meat, diced

¹/₄ cup tomato paste

1 (14 ounce) can corn

1 (14 ounce) can red beans, drained

1 (15 ounce) can white kidney beans, drained

1 (15 ounce) can black beans, drained and rinsed

¹/₂ cup fresh cilantro, chopped

Mix water with flour, set aside.

Put the onions, celery, chilies, stock, tomatoes and spices in a large stock pot and bring to a boil. Add the chicken bouillon and hot sauce. Simmer together 30 minutes.

Add turkey and corn, continue to simmer. Add beans. Cook 5-10 minutes and check seasoning. Stir in flour and water mixture to thicken. Adjust salt, pepper and hot sauce to taste.

After kayaking in Weber Canyon, mountain biking in the foothills of Ogden or skiing the Olympic downhill at Snowbasin, Roosters 25th Street Brewing Co. is the perfect destination for great food and exceptional brews. Located in a 100 year-old building on downtown Ogden's Historic 25th Street, Roosters' atmosphere is upbeat, upscale and eclectic.

Tortilla Soup

SOUP BASE:

1	medium onion, diced
2	cloves garlic, minced
2	tablespoons cooking oil
2	(14½ ounce) cans tomatoes, puréed

3-4 cups chicken broth

2	teaspoons salt
2	teaspoons pepper

juice from 1 lemon

1	teaspoon ground cumin

your favorite hot sauce to taste

ADDITIONS:

1	pound boneless chicken or steak, seasoned as desired
1	bunch cilantro, cleaned and chopped
½	red onion, diced
1	cup Cheddar cheese, shredded
1	lime, cut in wedges
2	ripe tomatoes, diced
1	avocado, diced

sour cream

tortilla chips

Combine the onion, garlic and cooking oil in a 6-quart pot and cook over medium-high heat until soft, about 10 minutes. Add the remaining soup base ingredients to the pot and continue to heat for 15 minutes. Adjust the seasoning with hot sauce, salt and pepper.

Roast the chicken or grill the steak until done. Cut it into bite-size chunks.

Arrange the remaining ingredients (additions) in separate bowls.

To serve: Put the desired ingredients in your own bowl and top with the soup broth. Add hot sauce to taste.

Painting by: Shanna Kunz

New England Clam Chowder

2 cups potatoes, diced
1 cup celery, chopped
1 cup onions, diced
4 (6½ ounce) cans chopped clams, drained; reserving juice
1 quart 2% milk
6 tablespoons butter
¾ cup flour
½ teaspoon sugar
1 teaspoon salt
dash of pepper
2 tablespoons Wondra® or all-purpose flour

Put potatoes, celery and onion in large pot. Pour clam juice over vegetables. Add just enough water to cover and simmer about 15-20 minutes or until tender.

In a saucepan, melt butter. Stir in flour, salt, pepper and sugar. Stir continuously until smooth. Add milk to saucepan and stir until very, very thick. Finish with Wondra® or flour for extra thickness.

Add mixture from saucepan to vegetables and blend. Stir in chopped clams and heat through.

Yield: 8½ cups

Mexican Chicken Corn Chowder

1½ pounds boneless, skinless chicken, diced
½ cup onion, chopped
1-2 garlic cloves, minced
3 tablespoons butter
1 cup chicken broth
½ teaspoon cumin
2 cups half-and-half
2 cups Monterey Jack or Pepper Jack cheese, shredded
1 can creamed corn
1 (4 ounce) can diced green chilies, not drained
1 can tomatoes, diced
¼ teaspoon Tabasco® sauce

Brown chicken, onion and garlic in butter in a 6-quart pot. Add broth and cumin, bring to a boil. Reduce heat, cover and simmer for 5 minutes.

Add remaining ingredients. Heat until cheese is melted.

Spinach Pear Salad

SALAD:

3   medium ripe yellow pears,
    unpeeled

3   cups baby spinach

2   tablespoons blue cheese,
    crumbled

1/4 cup chopped walnuts, toasted

DRESSING:

2   tablespoons balsamic vinegar

3   tablespoons olive oil

3   tablespoons orange juice

salt to taste

1   clove garlic, crushed

Core pears, cut length-wise in slices into a salad bowl. Add the spinach and cheese. Pour dressing over the salad and toss together lightly. Toast the walnuts at 350 degrees for 5 minutes. Sprinkle warm walnuts over the tossed salad.

Whisk together dressing ingredients and salt to taste.

Servings: 4

Dining Car Special
BROCCOLI SALAD

1/2 cup mayonnaise

1/4 cup sugar

1   tablespoon vinegar

1   bunch broccoli
    (buds and tender
    stalks)

1/2 sweet onion,
    chopped

1/2 pound bacon, fried
    and crumbled

1/2 cup grated Cheddar
    cheese

Make salad dressing by combining mayonnaise, sugar and vinegar. Dressing can be used immediately, but is best if allowed to sit for 3-4 hours. Chop broccoli into bite-sized pieces. Add onion, bacon and cheese. Toss with salad dressing.

Servings: 4-6

Strawberry & Kiwi Green Salad

1   (5 ounce) bag mixed greens
8   strawberries, sliced
3   kiwi, peeled and sliced in wedges
$^1/_2$ cup blue cheese, crumbled
$^3/_4$ cup pecans, large chunks, toasted

Toss mixture of greens (spring mix, spinach, iceberg and/or red leaf lettuce).

Top with sliced strawberries, kiwi wedges, blue cheese crumbles and large chunks of toasted pecans. Pass or drizzle dressing at serving time or toss greens with dressing just before serving and then top with fruit, nuts and cheese for nice presentation.

Sweet & Sour Salad Dressing

$^2/_3$ cup vegetable oil
6   tablespoons sugar
2   tablespoons sour cream
2   teaspoons Dijon mustard
$^1/_4$ cup rice vinegar

Mix all ingredients with a whisk. Refrigerate until ready to use.

Spinach, Pear & Green Bean Salad with Riesling Dressing

SALAD:

¹/₂   cup cored ripe Bartlett pear, peeled and diced

6   tablespoons medium-dry Riesling

3   tablespoons fresh lemon juice

1   tablespoon chopped shallot

1   teaspoon Dijon mustard

¹/₂   cup vegetable oil

¹/₂   pound haricots vert or small green beans, trimmed

6   cups packed baby spinach leaves (about 6 ounces)

3   ripe Bartlett pears, quartered, cored, cut into ¹/₄-inch thick slices

GARNISH:

³/₄   cup blue cheese, crumbled

³/₄   cup walnuts, toasted

salt and pepper to taste

Purée diced pear, Riesling, lemon juice, shallot and Dijon mustard in food processor until smooth. With machine still running, gradually add vegetable oil through feed tube and blend mixture until smooth. Transfer to bowl. Season dressing to taste with salt and pepper.

Cook green beans in large pot of boiling water until just tender but still firm to bite. Drain well. Transfer beans to medium bowl filled with ice water and cool thoroughly. Drain well. (Dressing and beans can be prepared a day ahead. Cover separately and refrigerate.)

Toss green beans, spinach and sliced pears in large bowl with enough Riesling dressing to coat. Sprinkle with crumbled blue cheese and toasted walnuts. Serve.

Cucumber Salad with Pineapple & Jalapeño

$^3/_4$ cup sugar

$^2/_3$ cup white vinegar

2   tablespoons water

$^1/_2$ teaspoon salt

1   cup fresh pineapple, peeled cored and cut into $^1/_3$-inch pieces

1   cucumber, cut into $^1/_3$-inch pieces

1   carrot, peeled, cut into matchstick-size strips

$^1/_3$ cup red onions, thinly sliced

1   tablespoon jalapeño, seeded and minced

1   tablespoon sesame seeds, toasted

lettuce leaves

Bring first 4 ingredients to boil in heavy small saucepan, stirring until sugar dissolves. Simmer until reduced to $^2/_3$ cup, about 4 minutes. Transfer syrup to large bowl and refrigerate until cold.

Add pineapple to syrup. Cover and refrigerate 1 hour. Add cucumber and next 3 ingredients to pineapple mixture; stir to coat. Line plates with lettuce leaves. Spoon salad atop lettuce. Sprinkle with sesame seeds and serve.

This recipe can be prepared in 45 minutes or less but requires additional sitting time.

Suggestion: Serve this salad as a fiery first course for an Asian-style entreé such as a stir-fry, or use it as a side dish for grilled chicken or fish.

Servings: 6-8.

Peach & Spinach Salad

$^1/_2$ pound fresh spinach, washed, trimmed and torn

1   purple onion, thinly sliced

1-2 fresh peaches, peeled and sliced

1   cup washed fresh bean sprouts

poppy seed dressing (see page 71)

Combine spinach, onion, peaches and sprouts. Toss with desired amount of dressing.

Utah Jazzy Blueberry Salad

SALAD BASE:

2   small boxes grape Jello®

2   cups hot water

1   (2 pound) can crushed
    pineapple

1   can blueberry pie filling

TOPPING:

1   (8 ounce) package cream
    cheese, softened

¹/₂   pint sour cream

¹/₂   cup sugar

1   teaspoon vanilla

Dissolve Jello® in water. Add pineapple and pie filling. Refrigerate until gelatin is set.

To make topping: Mix softened cream cheese and sour cream. Add sugar and vanilla. Beat until stiff.

Spread on Jello® and chill.

Mandarin Orange Jello® Salad

1   (6 ounce) package lemon
    pudding (not instant)

1   (6 ounce) package orange
    Jello®

1   cup boiling water

³/₄   cup cold water

1   (8 ounce) container whipped
    topping

2   small cans mandarin oranges

Prepare lemon pudding as directed on package. Add orange Jello® to boiling water until dissolved, then add cold water. Combine lemon pudding and orange Jello® until mixed throughout. Reserve 1 cup of mixture for topping, let set at room temperature. Pour into 9x13-inch pan and refrigerate until set. Combine whipped topping, mandarin oranges and reserved mixture. Spread on top of cooled salad and serve.

Cranberry Spinach Salad

2 bags baby spinach leaves
$^3/_4$ cup cranberries, dried
$^3/_4$ cup walnuts, coarsely chopped
2 red apples, diced (do not peel)
raspberry dressing

Toss together spinach, cranberries, walnuts and apples. Just before serving toss with raspberry dressing.

Servings: 10

Crunchy Romaine Salad

DRESSING:
1 cup sugar
$^3/_4$ canola oil
$^1/_2$ cup red wine vinegar
1 tablespoon soy sauce,
or to taste
salt and pepper to taste

SALAD:
1 (3 ounce) package ramen
noodles
1 cup chopped pecans
$^1/_4$ cup unsalted butter
1 bunch broccoli, coarsely
chopped
1 head romaine, washed, dried
and torn into bite-size pieces
4 green onions, chopped

Combine the sugar, oil, vinegar, soy sauce, salt and pepper in a jar with a tight-fitting lid. Shake until blended. Break the ramen noodles into small pieces, discarding the flavor packet. Brown the noodles and pecans in the butter in a skillet. Drain on paper towels. Let stand until cool. Combine the noodles, pecans, broccoli, romaine and green onions in a salad bowl and mix gently. Add 1 cup or more of the dressing, tossing to coat.

Snow Pea Salad

1/4 teaspoon white pepper

1/4 teaspoon kosher salt

1 cup mayonnaise

1 cup sour cream

2 (1 pound) bags frozen petite peas

15 snow peas, cut in half

1/2 red onion, minced

1 (3 ounce) jar bacon bits

1 (5 ounce) can water chestnuts, minced

Mix together pepper, salt, mayonnaise and sour cream. Set aside.

Lay the frozen peas out on paper towel, let them thaw and dry out, blot and put in large salad bowl. Clean and string snow peas and add to bowl. Combine the remaining ingredients.

Blend in dressing and refrigerate a minimum of 4 hours before serving.

Servings: 8-12

Spinach Salad

SALAD:

1 head iceberg lettuce, chopped

1 package baby spinach

8 ounces mushrooms, thinly sliced

1-2 cups Swiss cheese, shredded

1/2-1 pound bacon, cooked and chopped

Optional: red onion, thinly sliced

DRESSING:

1 cup vegetable oil

1/2 cup red wine vinegar

1/2 cup sugar

1/2 cup green onions, sliced

1/2 teaspoon dry mustard

1 teaspoon salt

1 tablespoon poppy seeds

In a large bowl toss together lettuce, spinach, mushrooms, Swiss cheese, bacon and (optional) red onion; refrigerate.

Prepare dressing by mixing oil, vinegar, sugar, green onions, dry mustard, salt and poppy seeds.

Just before serving, toss salad with desired amount of dressing.

Rainbow Pepper Salad

2   green peppers

2   sweet red peppers

1   yellow pepper

1   purple onion

¹/₃   cup vegetable oil

2   tablespoons tarragon vinegar

1   tablespoon Dijon mustard

2   teaspoons sugar

1   teaspoon salt

¹/₄   teaspoon freshly ground
     pepper

¹/₄   teaspoon Tabasco® sauce

1   jalapeño pepper, minced

1   teaspoon lime zest

Cut peppers and onion into julienne strips. Set aside. Combine oil, vinegar, Dijon mustard, sugar, salt, pepper and Tabasco® sauce in a large bowl. Beat with whisk until thick. Add peppers, onion, jalapeño and lime zest and toss gently. Cover and refrigerate for 3 hours before serving.

Cilantro & Tomato Salad

SALAD:

6   tomatoes, mixed varieties,
     yellow, cherry, plum, etc.

¹/₂   cup sweet onion, thinly sliced

¹/₄   cup cilantro, chopped

1   teaspoon jalapeño pepper,
     minced

2   garlic cloves, minced

DRESSING:

2   tablespoons vegetable oil

1   tablespoon rice vinegar

1   teaspoon oriental sesame oil

1   teaspoon soy sauce

¹/₂   teaspoon kosher salt

Mix together tomatoes, sweet onion, cilantro, jalapeño pepper and garlic.

To make dressing: Mix oil, rice vinegar, oriental sesame oil, soy sauce and kosher salt.

Mix tomato mixture with dressing and serve.

Southern Slaw

DRESSING:

1/2 cup plus 1 tablespoon oil
1/4 cup sugar
1/4 cup pepper infused or apple
     cider vinegar
1   package chicken flavor from
     ramen noodles
1   package ramen noodles,
     broken
2   tablespoons vegetable oil

SALAD:

1   cup sunflower seeds
1   cup sliced almonds
1   package broccoli slaw
3   tablespoons green onions,
     chopped

Mix 1/2 cup oil, sugar, vinegar and flavor packet from noodles together. Continue mixing until sugar is dissolved. Set aside.

Toast sunflower seeds, almonds and ramen noodles in oil. Cool.

Mix broccoli slaw and green onions together. Combine with dissolved sugar mixture. Refrigerate at least 1 hour.

Stir in toasted mixture before serving.

Tomato & Bread Salad

3/4 pound day-old crusty bread
     cut into 1-inch cubes (about 6
     cups)
2   cloves garlic, mashed with 1
     tablespoon of coarse salt
2   large tomatoes (about 1
     pound), trimmed and each cut
     into about 8 wedges
3/4 cup cucumber, sliced
1/2 cup red onion, sliced
1/2 cup extra virgin olive oil
2   tablespoons balsamic vinegar
10   fresh basil leaves, shredded

In serving bowl, stir together bread, garlic, tomatoes, cucumber, onion, oil, vinegar and basil. If your bread isn't stale, toast it until lightly golden brown. Adjust seasonings as needed. Stir well. Let stand for 1 hour before serving.

Serves 4-6

Mendocino Goat Cheese Salad

3   cups romaine, endive mix
$^1/_2$ cup almonds
$^1/_4$ cup olive oil
cayenne or chile pepper
4   ounces goat cheese

Wash lettuce and place on individual plates. Sauté whole almonds in olive oil in a skillet, add cayenne or chile pepper. Remove almonds and place a small amount on the side of each plate. Make $1^1/_2$-2-inch round patties of goat cheese. Shape and put into skillet and lightly brown on both sides (use low heat to warm but not melt cheese). Place 2 patties on lettuce and drizzle remaining hot olive oil from skillet over the top. Serve immediately while still warm.

Oasis Lentil Salad

SALAD:

1   pound small green lentils
1   large onion, thinly sliced
1   green pepper, sliced
1   red pepper, sliced
2   tomatoes, chopped
salt to taste

MARINADE:

$^3/_4$ cup olive oil
3   tablespoons lemon juice
$^1/_3$ cup cider vinegar
1   clove garlic, minced
$^1/_3$ teaspoon black pepper
$2^1/_2$ teaspoons salt
$^1/_4$ teaspoon cayenne pepper
1   teaspoon ground cumin
$^1/_2$ teaspoon thyme
$^1/_2$ teaspoon dry mustard
6   ounces kalamata olives, pitted
    and sliced

Boil lentils until al denté, rinse in cold water, drain.

Combine marinade ingredients and pour over lentils, let stand in refrigerator for at least an hour or more.

Let lentils come to room temperature. Combine with onion and peppers. Serve in a large bowl garnished with tomatoes. Add salt to taste.

Candied Walnut Salad

TOPPING:

1   cup sugar

$^1/_3$ cup water

1   tablespoon vanilla

1   pound of walnuts

VINAIGRETTE:

$^1/_4$ cup sugar

$^1/_3$ cup cider or white vinegar

1   teaspoon dry mustard

1   teaspoon salt

1   cup canola oil

SALAD:

1   pound of mixed greens or fresh spinach

$^1/_2$ cup Craisins®

$^1/_2$ cup caramelized walnuts (from topping above)

4-6 ounces blue/Gorgonzola cheese, crumbled

$^1/_2$ cup red onion, thinly sliced

To make topping: In a large pan combine sugar, water and vanilla. Cook over medium heat until sugar is dissolved and golden brown in color. Add walnuts, coating evenly with sugar mixture. Lay nuts on a cookie sheet to set. May be frozen at this point for future use.

To make vinaigrette: Combine sugar, vinegar, dry mustard and salt with canola oil. Mix for 2-3 minutes. Refrigerate.

Combine salad ingredients in a medium bowl and toss salad with vinaigrette. Sprinkle with walnut topping.

Mandarin Chicken Salad

1   (6 ounce) can frozen orange
    juice concentrate
1   cup pineapple juice
6   ounces soy sauce
2   garlic cloves, minced
$^1/_2$ teaspoon fresh ginger, peeled
    and minced
2   whole chicken breasts
    (boneless, skinless)
$^1/_2$ package wonton skins
vegetable oil or peanut oil
4   ounces almonds, slivered,
    toasted
1   bunch green onions, julienne
1   cup fresh cilantro leaves

MANDARIN DRESSING:
reserved chicken marinade
2   tablespoons hoisin sauce
1   teaspoon oriental sesame oil
2   tablespoons lemon juice
1   teaspoon dry mustard

In a small bowl combine the orange juice, pineapple juice, soy sauce, garlic and ginger. Pour over chicken and marinate for several hours or overnight in refrigerator.

Bake chicken in marinade at 350 degrees for 25 minutes or until just springy to the touch. Turn once during cooking. When cool, remove the chicken and reserve marinade. Shred and set aside. Cut wonton skins in $^1/_2$-inch strips and fry in the oil until crisp. Toss chicken, wontons, almonds, onions and cilantro together.

Skim fat from the reserved marinade. Add to dressing and boil all ingredients gently to blend flavors. Cool. Pour over salad and toss.

Servings: 6-8

Suggestion: Serve on a bed of lettuce.

Note: The combination of the orange juice and cilantro makes this salad truly distinctive.

Chinese Chicken Salad

1/3 cup vegetable oil
1/3 cup rice vinegar
4 teaspoons sugar
1 teaspoon red pepper, crushed
dash or 2 of soy sauce
2 teaspoons sesame oil
1 package ramen noodles
1/2 cup almonds, slivered
1/4 cup sesame seeds
1 package of shredded cabbage
6 chicken breasts, cooked, chopped
1/2 cup green onions, sliced
celery and cilantro to taste, chopped

Mix vegetable oil, rice vinegar, sugar, crushed red pepper and soy sauce. Refrigerate for 24 hours.

Crunch ramen noodles in their bag (discard seasoning packet).

In sesame oil, fry noodles, almonds and sesame seeds. Set aside.

In large bowl, combine cabbage and fried mixture. Add the chicken, green onions, celery and cilantro. Pour dressing over salad and serve.

Servings: 5-6

Taco Salad

1 pound ground beef
1 medium onion, chopped
1 tablespoon ground cumin (or 1 packet taco seasoning)
1/2 cup plus 2 tablespoons prepared salsa
1/2 teaspoon salt
1 (15-16 ounce) can kidney beans, rinsed and drained
1 small head lettuce, chopped or shredded
2 tomatoes, chopped
2 cups coarsely chopped corn chips
1/3 cup mayonnaise
1 avocado, peeled and diced
1/2 cup Cheddar cheese, shredded

Brown meat, onion and cumin (or taco seasoning) in 10" skillet, drain. Add 1/2-cup salsa and salt; mix well. Stir in beans and heat through. In a large mixing bowl, combine lettuce, tomatoes and corn chips. Combine mayonnaise and remaining salsa. Pour over lettuce mixture and toss well. Place lettuce mixture on serving platter or in a large shallow bowl. Top with beef mixture.

Garnish with avocado, cheese and additional corn chips.

Servings: 6

Warm Noodle Salad with Beef & Beans

1   pound fresh Chinese noodles or ³/₄ pound linguine

³/₄ pound London broil or other steak, thinly sliced

1   tablespoon oyster sauce

2   teaspoons reduced sodium soy sauce

1¹/₂ teaspoons chili paste with garlic

3   garlic cloves, finely chopped

1   tablespoon peanut oil

¹/₂ pound green beans, trimmed

¹/₂ cup chicken broth, defatted

4   scallions, trimmed, slivered and cut in 3-inch lengths

12   cherry tomatoes, halved

4-6 cups mixed salad greens

Cook noodles in large pot of boiling salted water until just tender. Drain and rinse thoroughly to cool.

Combine meat with oyster sauce, soy sauce, chili paste and garlic in medium sized bowl. Heat oil in large wok. Add beef mixture and green beans to wok. Stir-fry until meat is just browned, about 2 minutes. Add broth and cover. Steam until beans are tender, about 2 minutes. Remove wok from heat. Stir in noodles, scallions and tomatoes.

To serve, arrange greens in large salad bowl or individual salad plates. Mound warm salad on top. Serve at once.

Servings: 4-6

Pasta Salad with Roasted Asparagus

1¹/₂ pounds asparagus, trimmed
    and cut diagonally into 1-inch
    pieces
1   red or yellow bell pepper,
    cored, seeded and cut into
    1-inch strips
3   tablespoons olive oil
coarse salt
¹/₂ pound pasta, spirals or twists
1-2 tablespoons fresh herbs (basil,
    oregano or thyme), chopped
1   tablespoon lemon juice
freshly ground black pepper to
    taste

GARNISH:
¹/₄ cup toasted pine nuts or sprigs
    of fresh herbs (optional)

Preheat oven to 500 degrees and begin heating large pot of boiling salted water for pasta.

Combine asparagus and peppers in large mixing bowl. Toss with 2 tablespoons olive oil. Spread on baking sheet and sprinkle with coarse salt. Roast for about 7 minutes, until asparagus is tender when pierced with fork. Return to bowl. Stir to cool.

Cook pasta until done. Drain and rinse thoroughly to cool. Toss with vegetables, along with remaining 1 tablespoon olive oil, lemon juice and fresh herbs. Season to taste with pepper and additional salt or herbs, if needed.

Garnish with pine nuts or fresh herbs if desired. Serve at once.

Servings: 4-6

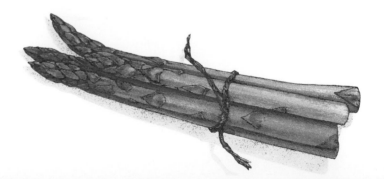

Tortellini Salad

14 ounces dried cheese tortellini

$^1/_3$ cup olive oil

$^1/_4$ cup garlic-flavored red wine vinegar

2 tablespoons Worcestershire sauce

1 tablespoon Dijon-style mustard

$1^1/_2$ teaspoons pepper, coarsely ground

1 large garlic clove, minced

2 tablespoons sugar

2 teaspoons salt

2 dashes Tabasco® sauce

1 cup celery, thinly sliced

1 cup green onion, chopped (both tops and bottoms)

1 cup mushrooms, thinly sliced

1 cup aged Cheddar cheese or feta, crumbled into small pieces

GARNISH:

2 tablespoons Italian or regular parsley, minced

In large pot, cook tortellini in boiling water until al denté. Drain and rinse in cold water. Transfer to medium-size bowl and toss thoroughly with olive oil. In another bowl, mix vinegar, Worcestershire sauce, mustard, pepper, garlic, sugar, salt and Tabasco®, blending well. Add celery, green onions, mushrooms and cheese and mix well again. Combine with tortellini in large bowl. Toss well and marinate 8-24 hours in the refrigerator, tossing frequently.

Three hours before serving, remove salad from refrigerator and toss occasionally.

Serve at room temperature, garnished with parsley.

Servings: 6

Sweet Onion Potato Salad

3   pounds medium-sized red
    potatoes
1   large sweet onion or other
    mild onion, thinly sliced
1   cup celery, thinly sliced
1   large golden delicious apple,
    peeled and diced
12 pimiento-stuffed Spanish style
    olives, thinly sliced
1/3 cup sweet pickle, chopped; or
    pickle relish
1 1/2 cups mayonnaise
1   teaspoon Dijon mustard
2   tablespoons distilled white
    vinegar
1   teaspoon bottled steak sauce
    or soy sauce
salt and pepper to taste

In a 4-5 quart pan, place potatoes in 1-inch of boiling water, cover and boil over medium heat until tender when pierced, 25-30 minutes. Drain well and let cool. Peel potatoes; place in large bowl.

Cut onion into quarters and slice thin; add to potatoes along with celery, apple, olives and pickle.

In a small bowl, stir together mayonnaise, mustard, vinegar and steak sauce. Spoon over potato mixture and mix gently. Season to taste with salt and pepper. Cover and refrigerate for at least 2 hours or overnight.

Servings: 10-12

Summer German Potato Salad

8   large red potatoes
1   pound bacon
9   hard boiled eggs
1   medium onion, chopped
1   cup mayonnaise
1   clove garlic, pressed
salt, pepper, vinegar to taste

Cut potatoes into bite-size pieces and boil until tender; drain. Fry bacon until very crisp; crumble and set aside. Slice eggs and onions. Combine potatoes, eggs, bacon, onion and mayonnaise. Season to taste with garlic, salt, pepper and a dash of vinegar. Serve at room temperature.

Fresh Oregano and Honey Dijon Dressing

6   tablespoons olive oil
2   tablespoons honey
2   tablespoons red wine vinegar
2   garlic cloves, minced
2   tablespoons fresh oregano,
     finely chopped
1/2 teaspoon Dijon mustard
1   red onion, chopped

Whisk first 6 ingredients together in a bowl. Add red onion, stir to blend. Dress salad greens and serve.

Great Salad Dressing

1/8 cup vegetable oil
2   tablespoons red wine vinegar
1   garlic clove, minced
2   tablespoons soy sauce
3   tablespoons milk
4   tablespoons mayonnaise
1   teaspoon dry mustard

Combine all ingredients in a jar and shake. Serve over green salad.

Poppy Seed Dressing

2   teaspoons dry mustard
1 1/2 cup sugar
2/3   cup white vinegar
2   teaspoons salt
3   tablespoons onion juice (in
      jar or juice from freshly grated
      onion)
2   cups vegetable oil
3   tablespoons poppy seed

Mix sugar, mustard, salt and vinegar. Add onion juice and stir slowly. Add oil. Beat constantly until thick (at least 5 minutes). Add poppy seed.

Notes:

Colorful Complements

Painting by: Marama H. Hansen

Summer Saturdays in Ogden take on a delicious appeal. From July through October you can get your fill of fresh produce, delicious food and fine art at the Farmers' Market, located in the Municipal Park Gardens on Historic 25th Street. The park sizzles with live bluegrass, folk and rock. The park and gardens are also home to Ogden's beautiful new amphitheater, which hosts summer concerts, family movies and more. During the holidays, the park becomes a magical place. Ogden's Christmas Village, a long-standing tradition in Weber County, lights up with beautiful displays, music and of course… Santa!

Local businesses sponsor miniature cottages including replicas of Union Station, the Municipal Building and Peery's Egyptian Theatre. In commemoration of its 50th Anniversary, Junior League of Ogden contributed a cottage, which celebrates its commitment to the community.

It is rumored that Butch Cassidy spent some time in Ogden and rented rooms in the Broom Hotel on 25th Street. It is said that in 1896 he and some of his men spent time along the Weber River bottoms calculating how they might break a friend out of jail.

SAVORY SIDE DISHES

Wild Rice with Peppers & Roasted Pecans

¹/₂ cup pecans, coarsely chopped

1 tablespoon unsalted butter, melted

¹/₂ teaspoon dried thyme, crumbled

¹/₈ teaspoon salt

2 tablespoons olive oil

¹/₂ cup onion, sliced

¹/₂ red bell pepper, cut into julienne strips

¹/₂ yellow bell pepper, cut into julienne strips

³/₄ cup uncooked wild rice, thoroughly rinsed

¹/₂ cup long-grain rice

2¹/₄ cups chicken broth

salt and freshly ground black pepper to taste

Preheat oven to 375 degrees. In small baking dish, combine pecans, butter, thyme and salt. Toss to coat. Bake 8 minutes or until crisp. Remove from oven and set aside. In large skillet, heat olive oil over medium heat. Add onion and bell peppers and cook until just soft, about 5 minutes. Remove from pan with slotted spoon and set aside. Add rice to same skillet and cook 1 minute, stirring constantly. Stir in chicken broth and heat to boiling. Season to taste with salt and pepper. Transfer to a large baking dish; cover and bake 30 minutes. Stir in onion mixture and cover; bake for 15 minutes or until rice is tender and liquid is absorbed. Just before serving, stir in reserved toasted pecans.

Servings: 4-6

Lemon Rice Pilaf

1   medium onion, minced

2   tablespoons butter or
      margarine

2   cups long grain rice, uncooked

29   ounces chicken broth

2   tablespoons lemon juice

1   teaspoon grated lemon zest

1   bay leaf

2   teaspoons fresh parsley,
      minced

2   tablespoons toasted pine nuts

salt and pepper to taste

In a large saucepan, sauté onion in butter for 3 minutes. Add rice, stirring to coat. Add broth, lemon juice, lemon zest and bay leaf. Heat to a boil and reduce heat to low. Cover and cook 15-20 minutes, or until liquid is absorbed. Remove from heat and let stand 5 minutes. Remove bay leaf. Stir in parsley and nuts. Season to taste with salt and pepper.

Servings: 6

Rice with Mushrooms

$2^2/_3$ cups Minute® rice (uncooked)

2   tablespoons onion, grated

2   ($14^1/_2$ ounce) cans beef broth

2   tablespoons soy sauce

6   tablespoons vegetable oil

1   small can mushrooms, drained

Combine all ingredients in an 8x8-inch casserole dish and bake at 350 degrees for 40 minutes.

Lowfat tip: reduce oil amount in half.

Arroz Verde (Green Rice)

$^1/_2$ cup fresh cilantro leaves,
   tightly packed
1   cup fresh stemmed spinach
   leaves, tightly packed
$1^1/_4$ cups chicken stock
$1^1/_4$ cups milk
1   teaspoon salt
1   tablespoon olive oil
3   tablespoons unsalted butter
$1^1/_2$ cups long-grain rice
$^1/_4$ cup onion, finely minced
1   clove garlic, minced

Put the cilantro, spinach and stock in a blender and blend until puréed. Add the milk and salt and blend until well combined. In a 3-quart, heavy-based saucepan with a good lid, heat the olive oil and butter over medium heat. When the butter is melted, add the rice and sauté, stirring about every 30 seconds until it begins to brown, 3-4 minutes. Add the onion and garlic. Cook one minute, stirring constantly. Add the contents of the blender and stir well. Bring to boil at high heat. Cover the pan and reduce heat to low; cook for 20 minutes. Stir the rice carefully to avoid crushing it, cover and cook another 5 minutes. Take the pan off the heat and let the rice steam in the covered pot for 10 minutes. Serve hot.

Crunchy Pecan Wild Rice

1   onion, finely chopped
1   cup pecans, chopped
4   tablespoons butter
1   teaspoon seasoning salt
4   cups cooked wild rice
2-3 tablespoons fresh parsley,
   minced

Sauté the onion and pecans in the butter in a skillet. Blend in the seasoning salt. Stir in the wild rice and cook until heated through. Adjust seasoning if desired. Sprinkle with parsley.

Servings: 6-8

Clay-Baked Black Beans

1¹/₃ cups black beans, dried
2 ounces smoked bacon, diced
¹/₂ tablespoon ground cumin
¹/₂ cup onion, finely chopped
¹/₂ cup red bell pepper, finely
   chopped
2 tablespoons poblano chili,
   seeded and minced
¹/₂ cup tomato, peeled, seeded
   and diced
1 bay leaf
2¹/₂ cups chicken stock
2 tablespoons cilantro leaves,
   minced
salt and pepper to taste

Place beans in a bowl, add water to cover by 2-inches and soak 4 hours, or overnight. Preheat oven to 300 degrees, unless you are using a clay pot that needs to be started in a cold oven. Add bacon to pan. Cook until starting to brown. Add cumin, onion, pepper and chili. Cook over medium heat until softened. Add tomato and cook until beginning to give up juices. Drain beans and add bay leaf and chicken stock. Transfer to ovenproof clay pot, cover and bake about 90 minutes until beans are very tender and still a bit soupy. Add more stock if needed. Season to taste. Fold in cilantro and serve.

Servings: 6

Spicy Green Beans

¹/₂ cup soy sauce
¹/₄ cup sesame oil
crushed red pepper flakes
1 clove garlic, minced
garlic salt
2 tablespoons black bean garlic
   sauce
1 tablespoon granulated sugar
¹/₄ teaspoon fresh ginger, peeled
   and grated
1 pound fresh green beans,
   snipped

Combine all ingredients except for beans. Set aside. Boil or blanch green beans. Marinate beans for at least 1 hour in spicy dressing. Serve at room temperature.

Curried Beans

1   onion, chopped
2   strips of bacon, chopped
1   red pepper, chopped
1   apple, peeled and diced
2   (27ounce) cans kidney beans
1   (27ounce) can stewed
    tomatoes
1   tablespoon curry powder
2   teaspoons salt
¹/₄ cup brown sugar, packed
¹/₄ cup Parmesan cheese, grated

Sauté onion, bacon and red pepper until soft. Mix all ingredients for about 1 hour on the stove (uncovered) to reduce the juices. Put in casserole dish and sprinkle the top with Parmesan cheese. Bake at 350 degrees until hot and bubbly.

Calico Beans

1   pound bacon
2   (15 ounce) cans pork and beans
1   (15 ounce) can lima beans,
    drained
1   (15 ounce) can butter beans,
    drained
1   (15 ounce) can kidney beans,
    drained
1   (15 ounce) can white beans,
    drained

SAUCE:
1   cup ketchup
1   cup brown sugar
2   teaspoons dry mustard
4   teaspoons vinegar
1   teaspoon salt
2   cups onions, diced
¹/₃ cup white sugar
4   tablespoons Worcestershire
    sauce

Fry bacon until crisp, then drain, chop and set aside. Saute onions in bacon drippings until tender, then rinse in metal strainer. Combine sauce ingredients and cook in crock pot on high until simmering; add beans. Turn crock pot to low setting and cook for 2-3 hours or bake at 350 degrees for 40 minutes.

Mashed Potatoes with Goat Cheese

3   pounds russet potatoes, peeled
    and cut into cubes
1   cup whole milk
1   onion, chopped
6   tablespoons (³/₄ stick) butter
4   ounces soft fresh goat cheese,
    crumbled

Cook potatoes in large pot of boiling salted water until tender, about 30 minutes. Meanwhile, bring milk, onion and butter to boil in small saucepan over medium high heat. Remove from heat.

Drain potatoes and return to pot. Add hot milk mixture and mash. Add goat cheese and mash until blended. Season to taste with salt and pepper (can be prepared 2 hours ahead). Let stand at room temperature. Before serving, stir over low heat until heated through.

Serve with beef or pork.

Servings: 6

Hollandaise Sauce

¹/₂   cup butter
4   egg yolks
¹/₄   cup fresh lemon juice
¹/₂   teaspoon salt
¹/₃   cup cream

Melt butter in a double boiler at low heat. In a separate bowl, mix egg yolks, lemon juice and salt. Add yolk mixture to melted butter at low heat and beat or whisk until thick. Add cream and continue whisking until thick. Do not overheat or sauce will curdle. If it curdles, cool immediately with a little more cream and whisk again. Keeps well in refrigerator.

Whipped Potatoes with Olive Oil & Parmesan

2 pounds russet potatoes, peeled and cubed
³/₄ cup canned chicken broth, hot
6 tablespoons olive oil
³/₄ cup Parmesan cheese, grated
¹/₂ cup fresh chives, chopped
salt and pepper to taste

Bring a large pot of water to boil. Add potatoes and cook until tender. Drain. Transfer to a large bowl; add broth. Beat potato mixture with an electric mixer until smooth. Gradually beat in oil, then Parmesan cheese, adding more broth if too thick. Stir in chives. Season with salt and pepper.

Garnish with additional grated cheese.

Roasted Potatoes with Asiago Cheese

16 tiny (1¹/₂-2-inch diameter red thin skinned potatoes, scrubbed
¹/₂ cup Asiago or Parmesan cheese, grated
¹/₂ cup mayonnaise
2 tablespoons green onion, minced
1 teaspoon paprika

Pierce potatoes in several places with a fork and put in a 9-inch round or square pan. Bake in a 375 degree oven until tender when pierced, about 1 hour. Let stand up in refrigerator until next day.

In a small bowl mix together cheese, mayonnaise and onion.

Cut each potato in half. Scoop a small cavity about ¹/₂ deep in each potato. Set potatoes aside in a 10x15-inch baking pan (you may trim a sliver off the rounded side of potatoes so they sit steady). Spoon cheese mixture equally into each. Dust liberally with paprika. Bake potatoes at 350 degrees until hot throughout, around 15 minutes. Place on platter and serve.

Bourbon Yams

5-6 yams
3-6 eggs
$^1/_4$ cup sugar
$^1/_2$ cup butter, melted
$^1/_2$ cup heavy cream
2 tablespoons bourbon
1 teaspoon vanilla

TOPPING:
$^1/_2$ cup melted butter
1 cup brown sugar
1 cup pecans, chopped
1 cup flour

Preheat oven to 350 degrees. Place yams in a buttered 2-quart casserole dish. Bake yams until done, about 30 minutes. Scoop out pulp and mash. Add eggs, sugar, butter, cream, bourbon and vanilla. Stir and pour into casserole dish. Mix topping ingredients together and sprinkle on top. Bake for 30 minutes.

Garnish with whole pecans.

Sweet Potato Pie

2 large sweet potatoes
1 egg, whole
2 eggs, separated
$1^1/_2$ cups milk
$1^1/_2$ cups sugar
1 tablespoon cornstarch
$^1/_2$ teaspoon vanilla
1 tablespoon margarine
1 teaspoon cinnamon
1 ready-made pie shell

Wash and peel potatoes, boil until cooked. Then mash potatoes. Mix in 1 whole egg, 2 egg yolks, milk, sugar, cornstarch, vanilla, margarine and cinnamon. Beat. Whip 2 egg whites and blend in with mixture. Pour into pie shell and bake slowly at 300 degrees until done.

Sweet Potato Puffs

2 pounds sweet potatoes

$^1/_3$ cup orange juice

1 egg, beaten

1 tablespoon grated orange zest

$^1/_2$ teaspoon ground nutmeg

$^1/_4$ cup pecans, chopped

Peel and cut sweet potatoes into 1-inch pieces. Place potatoes in medium saucepan. Add enough water to cover, bring to boil. Cook 10-15 minutes or until tender. Drain potatoes and place in large bowl. Mash until smooth. Add all ingredients except pecans mix well. Preheat oven to 375 degrees. Spray baking sheet with non-stick cooking spray. Spoon potato mixture into 10 mounds. Sprinkle pecans on top of mounds. Bake 30 minutes, or until centers are hot.

Scalloped Yams with Praline Topping

TOPPING:

$^1/_4$ cup brown sugar, packed

3 tablespoons butter, at room temperature

3 tablespoons all-purpose flour

$^1/_3$ cup pecans, finely chopped

SCALLOPED YAMS:

6 medium yams or sweet potatoes (about 3 pounds), peeled and cut into $^1/_2$-inch thick rounds

$1^1/_2$ cups heavy cream, heated

To make topping: Work together brown sugar, butter and flour in a bowl until well combined, then work in pecans. Set aside. (This topping can be prepared up to 8 hours ahead and kept at room temperature.)

To make scalloped yams: Bring a large pot of lightly salted water to a boil. Add yams and cook until crisp-tender, about 5 minutes. Do not overcook. Drain and rinse under cold running water. Preheat oven to 375 degrees. Lightly butter 9x13-inch baking dish. Arrange yams, overlapping in vertical rows, in dish. (This can be done up to 8 hours before baking, covered tightly with plastic wrap and refrigerated.) Pour cream over yams. Bake for 20 minutes. Crumble pecan mixture over yams and continue baking until yams are tender and topping is browned, 20-30 minutes longer.

Servings: 8-12

Roasted Tomato Risotto

1 1/2 cups Arborio rice
2-3 shallots, minced
1   tablespoon olive oil
1/2   cup white wine
6   cups chicken stock
6-8 roasted tomatoes, chopped
3-4 sprigs fresh thyme
3/4   cup Parmesan cheese, grated
2   tablespoons butter

Over medium heat, sauté shallots in olive oil until wilted. Add rice and cook until lightly toasted. Add wine and cook until absorbed. Add chicken stock a cup at a time until rice is done and risotto takes on a creamy texture. Add roasted tomatoes and thyme. Add butter and 1/2 cup Parmesan cheese right before serving.

Garnish with remaining Parmesan cheese.

Serves: 4-6

Cranberries with Dried Figs & Port

1 2/3 cups port
1/4   cup balsamic vinegar
1/4   cup packed brown sugar
8-10   dried Mission figs, chopped
1-2 sprigs fresh rosemary
1/4   teaspoon ground black pepper
1   (12 ounce) package fresh
     cranberries
3/4   cup sugar

Combine first 6 ingredients in medium saucepan. Bring to a boil, stirring until brown sugar dissolves. Reduce heat and simmer 10 minutes. Discard rosemary. Mix in cranberries and sugar. Cook over medium heat until cranberries burst, stirring occasionally. Cool and chill.

Pineapple with Basil

$^1/_2$ ripe pineapple (about 1 $^1/_2$ pounds)
1   teaspoon sugar
1   teaspoon fresh lemon juice, or to taste
2   tablespoons basil leaves, chopped
6   tablespoons orange liqueur or Grand Marnier® (optional)

Peel and core pineapple. Cut pineapple decoratively into bite-size pieces. In a large bowl, gently toss pineapple with sugar, lemon juice, chopped basil and optional orange liqueur or Grand Marnier®. Serve pineapple garnished with chopped basil.

Serves: 4

Three Onion Casserole

1   large purple onion, sliced
1   large white or yellow onion, sliced
1   bunch leeks, chopped
1   cup Havarti cheese, grated
1   package Boursin cheese, room temperature
1   cup Gruyére cheese, grated
4   tablespoons butter
$^1/_4$ cup white wine
salt and pepper to taste

Preheat oven to 350 degrees. Butter a medium size casserole dish. Thoroughly wash leeks in several changes of water and slice into $^1/_2$-inch size rounds, using the white and light green parts only. Place one third of the sliced onion and leeks in bottom of dish. Cover with Havarti cheese. Season with salt and pepper. Add another layer of onions and leeks, cover with Boursin cheese. Layer the last batch of onions and leeks with Gruyére cheese. Season with salt and pepper. Dot the top with 4 pats of butter. Add white wine over casserole and bake about 1 hour or until done.

Scorched Corn Pudding

7 cups frozen corn kernels

1 tablespoon butter or margarine

$^1/_4$ cup all-purpose flour

$2^1/_4$ cups low-fat milk

5 teaspoons sugar

$^1/_4$ teaspoon cayenne, or to taste

salt to taste

2 large eggs

2 large egg whites

In a 12-14-inch non-stick frying pan over high heat, stir corn often until about $^1/_4$ of the kernels are tinged with brown, 10-12 minutes. Add 1 tablespoon butter. When melted, add flour and mix well. Remove from heat and stir in milk, sugar and cayenne. Add salt to taste. In a small bowl, beat eggs and egg whites to blend. Stir in corn mixture. Butter a shallow 2 $^1/_2$ quart casserole (if desired, line with husks in a single layer; see notes). Pour in pudding. Bake in a 350 degree oven until center feels firm when lightly pressed, about 30 minutes (40-45 minutes if chilled).

Notes: Up to 1 day ahead, cover unbaked pudding and chill. For an attractive presentation, line the casserole with dried cornhusks, tips rising above the rim. Buy husks (available in 1 pound bags; husks keep indefinitely) in Mexican grocery stores and some supermarkets. Select 8-12 large husks, discard silks and cover with boiling water. Let stand about 30 minutes to soften. Drain and pat dry.

Servings: 10-12

Broiled Tomatoes with Olives and Garlic

2   medium vine-ripened
     tomatoes
3   Kalamata or other brine-cured
     black olives
1   large garlic clove
2   tablespoons olive oil
$^1/_4$ teaspoon salt
$^1/_4$ teaspoon black pepper, freshly
     ground

Preheat broiler. Cut tomatoes into $^1/_2$-inch thick slices. Oil a shallow baking pan large enough to hold tomatoes in one layer and arrange tomatoes in pan. Pit olives and chop fine with garlic. In a small bowl stir together olive mixture, oil, salt and pepper. Brush tomatoes evenly with mixture and broil about 3-inches from heat for 8 minutes, or until bubbling.

Servings: 2

Dining Car Special
DELUXE POTATO BALLS

2   pounds potatoes (3-4 large)
3   ounces cream cheese
$^1/_4$ cup milk
$1^1/_2$ teaspoons butter, chopped
1   tablespoon green onion,
     chopped
$^1/_4$ cup Parmesan cheese, grated
$2^1/_2$ teaspoons instant onion soup
     mix
$^1/_2$ teaspoon pepper
$^1/_2$ teaspoon salt
$^1/_2$ teaspoon seasoned salt
dash Tabasco® sauce
1   egg, beaten
$1^1/_2$ cups corn flakes, crushed

Peel the potatoes and cook in boiling water until tender. Drain and mash. Add the cream cheese, milk, butter, green onion, Parmesan cheese, onion soup mix, salt, pepper, seasoned salt and Tabasco® to the potatoes and mix well. Using an ice cream scoop dipped in water, form the potato mixture into balls. Dip each ball in beaten egg, roll in corn flakes and place on a greased baking sheet. Bake in a preheated 400 degree oven 10-15 minutes or until the potato balls are hot and crisp.

Servings: 16-20

Notes:

Master Strokes

ENTICING ENTREES

Painting by: David W. Jackson

Nestled between the Great Salt Lake to the west and the beautiful Wasatch Mountains to the east, Ogden was the site of the first white settlement in Utah; Fort Buenaventura. Surrounded by an outdoor paradise, there are plenty of places to camp within minutes of Ogden, whether you're pulling an RV or sleeping out under the stars. Five state parks and more than a dozen national forest areas are a short drive from the city. Without leaving Ogden, you can enjoy the 156-acre Ogden Nature Center. This urban oasis offers quiet walking trails, winter snowshoeing, excellent nature education programs and a wildlife rehabilitation center with hawks, owls and other protected species.

Painting by: Brandon Cook

ENTICING ENTREÉS

Portobello Pasta

2-3 cloves garlic, minced
1   large shallot, minced
2   tablespoons olive oil
1/4 cup prosciutto, chopped
2   large portobello mushrooms,
    chopped
1/3 cup Marsala wine
1   can chopped tomatoes
1   tablespoon rosemary, crushed
8   ounces penne pasta
Romano cheese to garnish
salt to taste

Boil water for pasta. Add 2 tablespoons salt to water. In sauté pan, sauté garlic and shallot in olive oil on medium heat until fragrant and wilted. Add prosciutto, then mushrooms. Cook 3-5 minutes, stirring constantly. Add Marsala and cook until most of the wine is evaporated. Add tomatoes, then cover pan and turn down heat. Meanwhile cook pasta. Drain and reserve 1 cup of cooking liquid from pasta, if sauce is dry add cooking liquid.

Toss cooked pasta, sauce and 1/2 herbs over high heat until sauce has a creamy consistency.

Garnish with remaining herbs and grated Romano cheese.

Linguine with Tomatoes & Basil

4   ripe large tomatoes, cut into
    1/2-inch cubes
1   pound Brie cheese, rind
    removed and torn into
    irregular pieces
1   cup cleaned fresh basil leaves,
    cut julienne
3   garlic cloves, peeled and finely
    minced
1   cup plus 1 tablespoon best-
    quality olive oil
2 1/2 teaspoons salt
1/2 teaspoon black pepper, freshly
    ground
8   ounces linguine or angel hair
    pasta
Parmesan cheese, freshly grated

Combine tomatoes, Brie, basil, garlic, 1 cup olive oil, 1/2 teaspoon salt and pepper in a large serving bowl. Prepare at least 2 hours before serving and set aside, covered, at room temperature.

Bring 6-quarts water to a boil in a large pot. Add 1 tablespoon olive oil and remaining salt. Add the linguine and boil until tender but still firm, 8-10 minutes. Drain pasta and immediately toss with the tomato sauce.

Garnish with freshly ground pepper and grated Parmesan cheese.

Servings: 4-6

Rigatoni & Meatballs

RIGATONI:

8 ounces rigatoni

8-9 cloves garlic, chopped fine

1-2 teaspoons olive oil

2 large cans tomato paste

salt and pepper to taste

$^1/_3$-$^1/_2$ cup sugar

MEATBALLS:

2-2$^1/_2$ pounds lean ground beef

6-8 cloves garlic, minced

2 large eggs

16 saltines, crumbled

$^1/_2$ cup fresh Parmesan cheese, grated

salt and pepper to taste

Brown garlic in oil. Add tomato paste and 6 cans of water. Add salt, pepper and sugar to taste. Simmer on stove or in crock-pot for 6 hours or until thick; add a little water and reduce heat.

Combine all meatball ingredients. Make into golf ball sized meatballs. Brown in frying pan or in oven. Add to sauce. Best if added 3 hours before serving. Serve over large rigatoni noodles. May be frozen for later use.

La Ferrovia's Spaghetti al Pomodoro

12-14 mature roma tomatoes

6 garlic cloves, minced

1 cup light olive oil

6-10 fresh basil leaves

1 pound spaghetti

salt and pepper to taste

Parmesan cheese, grated

Heat tomatoes in a pot of water until the tomatoes split. Drain water, let cool and then peel the tomatoes. In a 10-12-inch skillet, brown garlic in olive oil. Carefully add peeled tomatoes, salt and pepper to taste. Add 6-10 fresh basil leaves; simmer for approximately 15 minutes. Boil spaghetti and drain. Top with sauce and Parmesan cheese. For a quicker sauce, use 2 large cans of diced tomato in puree.

When Giuseppina and Rita Iodice left Naples, Italy, they brought with them their excellent authentic Italian recipes. Now, with the realization of their dream, it is their pleasure to share a bit of Italy with Ogden at La Ferrovia on Historic 25th Street.

Cheesy Mostaccioli

1   pound package mostaccioli
     pasta, cooked
1¹/₂ pounds ground beef, browned
     and drained
1   (11 ounce) can Cheddar
     cheese soup
1   (30 ounce) jar spaghetti sauce
1   teaspoon ground black pepper
1   teaspoon Italian seasoning
3   (12 ounces) cups mozzarella
     cheese, shredded

Preheat oven to 400 degrees. Combine pasta, meat, soup and spaghetti sauce. Add pepper, seasoning and 2 cups cheese. Mix to combine. Place in large baking dish. Sprinkle remaining cheese on top. Bake for 25 minutes until heated through.

Servings: 8-10

Easy Mac & Cheese

CREAM SAUCE:

¹/₄ cup butter
¹/₄ cup all-purpose flour
¹/₄ teaspoon salt
¹/₄ teaspoon pepper
2   cups half-and-half

MAC & CHEESE:

8   ounces uncooked macaroni
8   ounces Velveeta®

Heat butter until melted. Mix in flour, salt and pepper. Cook over low heat. Stir in half-and-half. Heat to boiling, stirring constantly. Boil and stir 1 minute. Remove from heat.

Heat oven to 350 degrees. Butter casserole dish. Cook macaroni as directed on package, drain. Prepare cream sauce. Stir in cheese. Heat over medium heat, stirring constantly, until cheese is melted. Layer ¹/₃ each of the macaroni and cheese. Repeat. Bake for 35 minutes.

Mexican Lasagna

1   (10 ounce) can enchilada
     sauce
1   (14 ounce) can chopped
     tomatoes
1   (6 ounce) can tomato paste
1   (16 ounce) can black beans,
     rinsed and drained
9   uncooked lasagna noodles
2   cups cottage cheese
3   cups sharp Cheddar cheese,
     shredded

Preheat oven to 375 degrees. Mix enchilada sauce, chopped tomatoes, tomato paste and black beans. Spoon $1/3$ of the sauce mixture over the bottom of a 9x13-inch pan. Top with 3 noodles. Spread 1 cup of cottage cheese and $2/3$ cup cheddar. Spoon $1/2$ of the remaining sauce over the top. Add another layer of noodles. Spread remaining cottage cheese and 1 cup of Cheddar. Add last 3 noodles. Cover with remaining sauce and sprinkle with Cheddar. Cover with foil and bake for 45 minutes or until noodles are tender. Let stand 5 minutes. Serve.

Lasagna

SAUCE:

1   pound Italian sausage
1   clove garlic, minced
1   tablespoon whole basil leaves
$1^{1}/_{2}$ teaspoons salt
2   (16 ounce) cans chopped
       tomatoes
2   (6 ounce) cans tomato paste
10   ounces lasagna or wide
       noodles

FILLING:

3   cups fresh Ricotta or creamy
       cottage cheese
$1/2$ cup Parmesan or Romano
       cheese, grated
2   tablespoons parsley flakes
2   beaten eggs
1   teaspoon salt
$1/2$ teaspoon pepper
1   pound mozzarella cheese,
       thinly sliced

Brown sausage slowly; spoon off excess fat. Add garlic, basil, salt, tomatoes and tomato paste. Simmer uncovered 30 minutes, stirring occasionally. Cook noodles al denté in salted, boiling water. Combine all remaining ingredients, except mozzarella cheese. Place half of the noodles in a greased 9x13-inch baking dish. Spread in layers using half of each ingredient: cottage cheese filling, mozzarella cheese and meat sauce. Repeat layers using the second half of the ingredients. Bake uncovered at 375 degrees for 30 minutes. Cover with foil and continue baking until bubbly. Let stand 10-20 minutes before cutting in squares (filling will set slightly). You can also prepare the lasagna early, refrigerate and then cook for 15 minutes longer.

Servings: 12

Creamy Fettuccini

4   tablespoons butter
4-6 garlic cloves, minced
4   cups heavy whipping cream
$^1/_4$ cup cooking sherry
8   ounces fettuccini
salt and pepper to taste

Sauté garlic in butter on low heat, but do not brown. Add cream and sherry. Simmer approximately 45-60 minutes, until reduced. Mix with cooked fettuccini noodles or tortellini. Shrimp or chicken may be added for a heartier meal. Add salt and pepper to taste.

Red Bell Pepper & Prosciutto Pasta

4   tablespoons olive oil
1   medium onion, chopped
2   large bell peppers (red, yellow and/or green), chopped
2-3 garlic cloves, pressed or chopped
2   cans Italian tomatoes (drain 1 can), chopped
$^1/_2$ cup fresh basil, chopped
$^1/_4$ teaspoon crushed red pepper flakes
1   teaspoon oregano leaves
2   whole bay leaves
4-6 slices prosciutto, sliced into $^1/_4$-inch strips
1   pound fettuccini or linguine

GARNISH:
$^1/_2$ cup fresh Parmesan, Asiago or Pecorino cheese
fresh parsley, chopped

Sauté onion, peppers and garlic cloves in olive oil until barely tender. Add both cans of chopped tomatoes, 1 can drained. Add basil, pepper flakes, oregano leaves, bay leaves and prosciutto. Reduce heat to medium and cook, uncovered, approximately 20 minutes. Salt and pepper to taste. Boil pasta; drain and place in a large serving bowl. Top with pepper sauce.

Garnish with cheese and parsley and serve.

Servings: 5-8

Gourmet Chicken Spaghetti

3 pounds chicken
8 ounces thin spaghetti
4 tablespoons flour
4 tablespoons butter
1 cup heavy cream
1 cup chicken broth
1 cup mayonnaise
1 cup sour cream
1 cup Parmesan cheese, grated
$^1/_3$ cup lemon juice
$^1/_3$ cup white wine
$^1/_2$ teaspoon garlic powder
$^1/_2$ teaspoon cayenne
1 teaspoon dry mustard
1 teaspoon salt
8 ounces fresh mushrooms, sliced
4 tablespoons butter
paprika

Boil and bone chicken. Break spaghetti into thirds and boil in chicken stock. Make basic white sauce. Melt butter; add flour and cook until bubbly. Add cream and chicken broth, stirring and cooking until thickened. Add mayonnaise, sour cream, Parmesan, lemon juice, wine and seasonings. Sauté mushrooms in butter. Place mushrooms, chicken and spaghetti in flat 3-quart casserole. Add sauce and mix well. Sprinkle paprika and additional Parmesan on top. Bake at 350 degrees for 30-40 minutes. May be made ahead of time and frozen.

Servings: 8-10

Spicy Chicken Pesto Pasta

2 tablespoons olive oil

1 pound skinless, boneless chicken breasts, cut into $^1/_3$-inch strips

3 green onions, thinly sliced

$^2/_3$ cup fresh cilantro, chopped

$^1/_3$ cup pecans, toasted and chopped

1 tablespoons garlic, minced

2 teaspoons seeded jalapeño, minced

$^1/_4$ teaspoon dried crushed red pepper

$^1/_2$ cup pesto

8 ounces linguine pasta

Heat oil in heavy large skillet over medium-high heat. Season chicken with salt and pepper. Add chicken to skillet and sauté until cooked through and beginning to brown, about 4 minutes. Using slotted spoon, transfer chicken to bowl. Add green onions, $^1/_3$ cup cilantro, pecans, garlic, jalapeño and dried red pepper to same skillet. Sauté until green onions wilt, about 2 minutes. Add pesto, chicken and any accumulated juices; stir to blend. Remove from heat.

Meanwhile, cook linguini in boiling salted water until tender but firm. Drain and reserve $^1/_4$ cup of liquid. Bring sauce to simmer. Add linguini and reserved liquid to sauce and toss to coat. Season to taste with salt and pepper. Transfer to a large bowl. Sprinkle with additional cilantro.

Servings: 4

Pasta with Peas, Crab & Basil

$^3/_4$ pounds of penne pasta

4 tablespoons unsalted butter

2 shallots, minced

$^1/_2$ cup white wine

1 cup chicken broth

$1^1/_2$ cups heavy cream

1 cup peas, fresh or frozen, roughly chopped

1 pound lump crabmeat, rinsed and picked over

$^1/_4$ cup basil, plus garnish, loosely chopped

salt and freshly ground pepper to taste

Bring a large saucepan of water to a boil and generously salt. Stir in pasta; cook until al denté. Transfer to a colander and drain.

Meanwhile, melt butter in large sauté pan over medium heat. Add shallots and cook until they are translucent and fragrant, about 2 minutes. Add wine and chicken broth and simmer for 5 minutes or until your liquid has reduced by about half. Add cream and bring back to a simmer. Add peas and season with salt and pepper; cook until peas are tender and bright green, 4-5 minutes. Add crab and continue cooking, stirring constantly, until it is heated through, about 1 minute more. Add the pasta and stir to combine.

Stir in chopped basil and remove from heat; season with salt and pepper. Divide among serving plates and garnish with basil. Serve immediately.

Servings: 6-8

Hungry Wolf Mediterranean Shrimp & Artichoke Pasta

24 large shrimp, cleaned and deveined

2 ounces vegetable oil

2 teaspoons fresh garlic, chopped

2 teaspoons fresh shallots, chopped

2 medium size ripe tomatoes (cut in $1/4$-inch chunks)

3 tablespoons capers

1 cup artichoke hearts, quartered

$1/4$ cup sliced black olives

8 ounces extra-virgin olive oil

6 ounces dry white wine

1 cup vegetable broth

$1/4$ cup fresh basil, chopped (do not mince, it will bruise)

2 tablespoons fresh parsley, chopped

3 cups cooked pasta (angel hair is best)

$1/3$ cup good quality Parmesan cheese, grated

In a large, hot, saucepan, sauté shrimp using the 2 tablespoons of vegetable oil. Do not over cook. Remove the shrimp and add the garlic and shallots. Cook gently until the garlic turns slightly golden color. Add tomatoes, capers, artichoke hearts, olives, olive oil, wine and vegetable broth and simmer for 2-3 minutes. Add the fresh herbs and shrimp. Pour evenly over the prepared cooked pasta and garnish with grated Parmesan cheese.

Servings: 4

The Hungry Wolf Grill at Wolf Creek Resort presents a spectacular view overlooking the entire upper Ogden Valley and incredible dining with a diverse menu to satisfy any palate.

Spicy Shrimp Linguine

16-20 shrimp, peeled and
    deveined
1   tablespoon sliced jalapeño
1   tablespoon olive oil
5   red onion rings
salt and pepper to taste
$^1/_2$ cup diced tomatoes
3   tablespoons cilantro, chopped
1   tablespoon lemon juice
2   ounces chicken broth
arrowroot (or flour)
9   ounces linguine, cooked
2   pieces garlic toast

PARMESAN HERB MIX:

$1^1/_2$ ounces Parmesan cheese,
    grated
green onion, chopped
red bell pepper, diced
cilantro, chopped
basil, chopped
parsley, chopped

Place shrimp, jalapeño, olive oil, onion, salt, pepper and tomato in a large sauté pan; sauté for 3-4 minutes. Add the cilantro and sauté for 1 minute. Add the lemon juice and chicken broth and sauté for 2 minutes. Thicken slightly with arrowroot; toss in the linguine and continue to heat for 1-2 minutes. Serve on a round plate with Parmesan herb mix and garlic toast.

Gorgonzola Sauce for Pasta

1 1/2 cups heavy whipping cream
3/4 cup crumbled Gorgonzola or other blue cheese
1/4 cup Parmesan cheese, freshly grated
pepper to taste

Bring cream to boil in heavy saucepan. Boil until thickened slightly, about 3 minutes. Add Gorgonzola, stir until melted. Season with pepper. Sprinkle with Parmesan cheese.

Bistro 258-Spicy Penne Pasta

1 tablespoon olive oil
1 medium red onion, thinly sliced
pinch of salt
small pinch of pepper or 2 turns of grinder
1/2 teaspoon garlic, finely chopped
1 rounded teaspoon crushed chili flakes
1 ounce vodka

1/2 cup heavy cream
3 cups favorite non-meat marinara or homemade Chianti marinara
1 pound penne pasta

GARNISH:
Parmesan cheese, grated
parsley, minced

Start large pot of pasta water boiling to use later. In large non-stick sauté pan add oil, red onions, salt and pepper and place on high heat. Cook until onions start to caramelize (brown slightly) flipping or stirring occasionally. Drop pasta into water, stirring occasionally. When onion is caramelized, add garlic, chili flakes and vodka, toss over heat for 1 minute to release flavors and oils. Add heavy cream and reduce until mixture is thick, add marinara and simmer until mixture is hot. Remove pasta from water and add to sauce and toss. Transfer to pasta bowls.

Garnish with Parmesan and parsley.

This award winning restaurant is found in the heart of Historic 25th Street. Simplicity of the name (258 is the address) fools the customer of its intimate ambience and decadent morsels served here.

Thai-Spiced Cilantro Chicken

4   full boneless chicken breasts
2   garlic cloves, peeled
1   fresh or canned green chili, seeded
3/4 inch piece fresh ginger, peeled
4   tablespoons fresh cilantro, chopped
zest of 1 lime
3   tablespoons lime juice
2   tablespoons light soy sauce
1   tablespoon superfine sugar
3/4 cup coconut milk

With a sharp knife cut 3 deep slashes into skinned side of each chicken breast. Place in non-metallic dish.

Put garlic, chili, ginger, cilantro, lime zest, lime juice, soy sauce, superfine sugar and coconut milk in food processor and process to a smooth puree. Spread puree over both sides of chicken coating evenly.

Cover dish and marinate in refrigerator for 1 hour. Lift chicken from marinade, drain off excess juice and place on baking sheet.

Broil under pre-heated broiler for 12-15 minutes, until thoroughly and evenly cooked. Place remaining marinade in saucepan and bring to boil. Reduce heat and simmer for several minutes, heating thoroughly. Serve with chicken breasts.

Margarita Chicken

4   boneless, skinless chicken breast halves
2   tablespoons corn oil
2   tablespoons lime juice
1   tablespoon honey
1   cup finely crushed tortilla chips
1   (14 1/2 ounce) can Mexican style stewed tomatoes
2   tablespoons chopped cilantro
1/3 cup grated Monterey Jack cheese

Brush chicken with mixture of oil, lime juice and honey. Roll chicken in tortilla chips to coat. Bake for 20-25 minutes at 325 degrees. While baking chicken, purée tomatoes and cilantro into a smooth sauce. Remove chicken from oven, top with puree and sprinkle with cheese. Return to oven and bake for 5 minutes or until cheese melts.

Garnish with cilantro and lime wedges and serve.

Servings: 4

Grilled Chicken &
Mushroom Quesadillas

½ stick butter
2½ teaspoons chili powder
2 garlic cloves, minced
1 teaspoon dried oregano
4 ounces fresh shiitake
   mushrooms, stemmed and
   sliced
1½ cups cooked chicken,
   shredded
⅔ cup onion, finely chopped
⅓ cup fresh cilantro, chopped
2½ cups Monterey Jack cheese,
   grated
olive oil
corn tortillas

Melt butter in large skillet over medium high heat. Add chili powder, garlic, oregano and mushrooms. Sauté until fragrant, about one minute. Remove from heat. Mix in chicken, onion and cilantro. Cool 10 minutes. Mix in cheese and season with salt and pepper. Can be made 8 hours ahead and chilled.

Prepare barbeque. Lightly brush oil on one side of 8 tortillas. Place tortillas, oil side down on large baking sheet. Divide chicken mix among tortillas, spread evenly. Top with remaining tortillas and brush with oil. Grill quesadillas about 3 minutes per side.

Sweet and Sour Chicken

½ onion, chopped
2 whole chicken breasts,
   (boned, skinned and cut into
   bite sized pieces)
3 tablespoons vegetable oil
6 tablespoons sugar
1½ tablespoons cornstarch
3 tablespoons cider vinegar
1 tablespoon soy sauce
½ teaspoon salt
2½ tablespoons ketchup
½ cup water
1 (8 ounce) can pineapple
   chunks, with juice
vegetables of choice, chopped

Stir-fry the onion and chicken in 1 tablespoon of oil until done. Add desired vegetables (bell peppers, carrots, etc.) and stir until tender crisp.

In another pan mix sugar and corn starch together. Add the vinegar, soy, oil, salt, ketchup and water. Cook over medium heat until thickened. Add pineapple chunks. Thicken a bit more. Pour over chicken mixture. Serve over steamed rice.

Fancy Fast Chicken

4-5 skinless, boneless chicken breasts

5 slices Swiss cheese

2 cups fresh mushrooms, sliced

1 (10 ³/₄ ounce) can cream of chicken soup

¹/₂ cup white wine

3 cups herb-seasoned stuffing mix

4 tablespoons melted butter

Place chicken in shallow baking pan lightly sprayed with cooking spray. Top each piece of chicken with cheese. Arrange mushrooms over cheese. In small bowl, combine soup and wine; pour over chicken. Sprinkle stuffing mix over the top and drizzle melted butter evenly over stuffing. Bake at 350 degrees for 45 minutes.

Servings: 4-5

Raspberry Chicken

6 boneless, skinless chicken breast halves or thighs (about 1¹/₂ pounds)

¹/₂ cup raspberry preserves, fruit-only type

¹/₂ cup frozen pineapple juice concentrate, thawed

¹/₂ cup soy sauce

2 tablespoons red wine vinegar

¹/₂ teaspoon chili powder

¹/₂ teaspoon curry powder

¹/₂ teaspoon garlic powder

¹/₄ cup fresh raspberries, mashed

¹/₄ cup fresh raspberries for garnish

white or wild rice, cooked

Place chicken in large baking pan. In small bowl, combine all ingredients except for garnish. Pour over chicken and cover tightly with foil. Marinate in refrigerator 2 hours or overnight. Preheat oven to 350 degrees. Bake (covered) 30-40 minutes. Remove from oven, transfer chicken to serving platter and top with pan juices.

Garnish with fresh raspberries. Serve over white or wild rice.

Servings: 6

Summer BBQ Chicken Tacos

8-12 chicken breasts, boned and
    skinned
1   cup fresh lime juice
1   cup white vinegar
1   cup corn oil
1   cup soy sauce
$^1/_2$ cup Worcestershire sauce
1   tablespoon salt
1   tablespoon pepper
1   tablespoon seasoned salt
2   teaspoons garlic powder
1   tablespoon sesame seeds
dash onion powder or green
    onions

Mix all ingredients. Reserve $^1/_4$ of the liquid for the tortillas. Pour over chicken and let marinate for 4 hours in the refrigerator and grill. Slice thin. Dip flour tortillas in reserved liquid and grill. Serve with accompaniments.

ACCOMPANIMENTS:
iceberg lettuce, shredded
diced tomatoes
grated cheese
guacamole
sour cream
salsa
flour tortillas

Painting by: Terry Johnson

Honeyed Chicken with Spicy Peanut Sauce

MARINADE:

6	tablespoons soy sauce
1	tablespoon honey
1	tablespoon coriander seed
2	cloves garlic, minced
2	teaspoons fresh ginger, peeled and finely grated
$^1/_4$	teaspoon turmeric
$^1/_4$	teaspoon cayenne pepper, or to taste
$2^1/_2$-3	pounds chicken breasts halved, thighs and legs separated

SPICY PEANUT SAUCE:

4	tablespoons peanut butter
4	tablespoons soy sauce
2	tablespoons fresh lemon juice
$^1/_4$	cup firmly packed brown sugar
$1^1/_2$	teaspoons cayenne pepper, or to taste
$^1/_4$	cup vegetable oil

In large bowl, combine all marinade ingredients. Mix well. Add chicken. Coat well. Marinate at room temperature 3 hours or in refrigerator overnight. Remove chicken from marinade. Broil or grill chicken over low heat, about 30 minutes until tender and browned, turning once. While chicken cooks, combine all sauce ingredients in food processor or blender. Process until smooth. In small saucepan, heat sauce briefly before serving with chicken.

Green Chicken Enchiladas

1 (18 ounce) package flour
  tortillas

FILLING:

1 cup Cheddar cheese, grated
2 cups Monterey Jack cheese,
  grated
2 cups cooked, cubed chicken
$^1/_2$ medium onion, chopped
$^1/_2$ cup sliced black olives
1 $^1/_2$ cups sour cream
2 tablespoons parsley, chopped
$^3/_4$ teaspoon pepper, freshly
  ground

SAUCE

2 tablespoons butter
2 tablespoons all-purpose flour
$^1/_2$ cup milk
1 $^1/_2$ cups chicken broth
1 (10 ounce) package frozen
  spinach, cooked, drained and
  coarsely chopped
$^2/_3$ cup sour cream
4 tablespoons green chilies,
  chopped
$^1/_2$ medium onion, chopped
1 clove garlic, minced
$^3/_4$ teaspoon cumin

GARNISH:

additional shredded cheese
lime slices
tomato slices

In a large bowl, mix together cheeses, chicken, onion, olives, sour cream, parsley and pepper and set aside.

In a sauté pan, heat butter over low heat. Add flour and cook for a few minutes, stirring constantly. Stir in milk and add $^1/_2$ cup chicken broth. Bring to a boil. Boil for 1 minute, stirring constantly. Add remaining chicken broth, cook and stir until hot and thickened, add spinach, sour cream, green chilies, onion, garlic and cumin.

Dip each tortilla into sauce, coating both sides. Spoon about $^1/_4$ cup filling onto each tortilla and roll up. Place seam-side down in an ungreased 9x13-inch baking dish. Pour remaining sauce over enchiladas and bake uncovered at 350 degrees for about 20 minutes or until bubbly.

Garnish with shredded cheese, lime and tomato slices. Serve.

Servings: 6-8

Lowfat Chicken Noodle Bake

1 cup 1% low-fat cottage cheese
$^1/_2$ cup light cream cheese
$^1/_2$ cup nonfat sour cream
$^1/_2$ cup low fat mayonnaise
$^1/_2$ cup chopped onion
$^1/_4$ cup fresh parsley, minced
2 tablespoons margarine
$^1/_3$ cup all-purpose flour
$^1/_2$ cup skim milk
1 (10$^1/_2$ ounce) can low-salt chicken broth
$^1/_2$ teaspoon poultry seasoning
$^1/_4$ teaspoon salt
$^1/_4$ teaspoon pepper
dash of garlic powder
9 cooked lasagna noodles
vegetable cooking spray
3 cups chicken breasts, cooked and diced
$^1/_2$ cup dry breadcrumbs
2 tablespoons fresh parsley, chopped
$^1/_4$ teaspoon paprika

Combine cottage cheese, cream cheese, sour cream and mayonnaise in a medium bowl; beat at high speed until well blended. Stir in onion and parsley; set aside.

Melt margarine in a medium saucepan over medium heat. Add flour and cook 1 minute, stirring constantly with a wire whisk. Gradually add milk and broth, stirring constantly. Bring to a boil over medium heat and cook 3 minutes or until thickened, stirring constantly. Stir in poultry seasoning, salt, pepper and garlic powder. Remove from heat; set sauce aside.

Arrange 3 noodles in bottom of a 9x13-inch baking dish coated with cooking spray. Top with half of the cottage cheese mixture, half of the chicken and half of the sauce. Repeat layers, ending with sauce. Combine breadcrumbs, 2 tablespoons of parsley and paprika; sprinkle over casserole. Bake uncovered at 375 degrees for 30 minutes. Serve immediately.

Servings: 8

Swiss Cheese Chicken

6-8 chicken breasts
6-8 Swiss cheese slices
2   (10 ³/₄ ounce) cans cream
     chicken soup
¹/₄ cup water
seasoned breadcrumbs

Arrange chicken breasts in a shallow baking dish. Place cheese on top of chicken. Combine soup and water; spoon over chicken. Sprinkle bread crumbs over top. Bake at 350 degrees for 50 minutes or until done.

Grilled Jamaican "Jerk" Chicken

10 boneless skinless chicken
     breasts
1   onion, diced
1   green pepper, diced
¹/₄ cup sugar
¹/₂ cup vegetable oil
2   teaspoons chili powder
2   teaspoons garlic powder
2   teaspoons onion salt
2   teaspoons basil
2   teaspoons thyme
2   teaspoons seasoned salt
2   teaspoons crushed red pepper
2   teaspoons cumin
2   teaspoons coriander
2   teaspoons ginger
2   teaspoons black pepper
1   teaspoon cinnamon
1   teaspoon ground cloves
1   teaspoon allspice
1   teaspoon cayenne
1   teaspoon salt

Pound chicken to tenderize. Mix onion, green pepper, oil, sugar and all seasonings in bowl; add chicken to marinate. Cover and refrigerate for 4 hours or overnight. Grill until just done. Do not overcook.

Servings: 10

Tex-Mex Stuffed Peppers

4   sweet red peppers

4   sweet yellow peppers

4   green bell peppers

2   whole chicken breasts, poached, skinned, boned and diced

6   scallions (green onions, white part and $^2/_3$ green), chopped

2   jalapeño peppers, seeded and diced

2   cloves garlic, minced

12   ounces cream cheese, room temperature

2   eggs

3   tablespoons heavy whipping cream

1   cup Monterey Jack cheese, grated

1   tablespoon ground cumin

2   cups canned chicken broth

salt and freshly ground black pepper to taste

Slice the tops from the peppers and pull out the seeds and cores. Dice 1 pepper and its top of each color and set aside. Reserve the other 9 tops as well. Drop the 9 remaining pepper shells into boiling salted water. Boil for 3 minutes. Drain and set aside. Combine the diced peppers and chicken in a mixing bowl. Add the scallions, jalapeño peppers and garlic and bind with the cream cheese by stirring with a wooden spoon. Stir in the eggs and cream, then the grated cheese. Season with the cumin, salt and pepper to taste. Preheat oven to 350 degrees. Place the pepper shells in a baking dish that will hold them snugly together. Spoon the filling into the peppers. Replace the tops and pour the broth around the peppers. Bake until the filling is puffed and the peppers are soft and wrinkled but still intact, about 1 hour. Serve immediately.

Servings: 8-9

Chicken and Dumplings

1   pound chicken breasts
1   cup flour
salt and pepper to taste
2   tablespoons of oil or
     shortening
1   onion, sliced
3-6 chicken bouillon cubes
1   cup celery, cut in 1-inch
     pieces
2   cups carrots, cut in 1-inch
     pieces

DUMPLING INGREDIENTS:
1   cup flour
1$^1/_2$ teaspoons baking powder
1   egg
$^3/_4$ teaspoon salt
$^1/_3$ cup milk

Dredge chicken in flour seasoned with salt and pepper. Brown the chicken in oil or shortening. Put into a baking pan and cover with water. Add 1 sliced onion, 3-6 chicken bouillon cubes. Cook slowly for a half an hour at 325 degrees. Add celery and carrots; cook another half an hour or until vegetables are done. Remove chicken from oven and add prepared dumplings.

Prepare dumplings by mixing egg, milk and dry ingredients. Spoon dumplings on top of chicken. Cover with tin foil and cook for 15 minutes. Then turn dumplings over and cook an additional 15 minutes.

Post-Thanksgiving Turkey Tetrazzini

6   tablespoons butter
5   tablespoons flour
2$^1/_2$ cups chicken broth
1$^1/_4$ cups half-and-half
$^1/_2$ cup dry white wine
$^1/_2$ cup Parmesan cheese, grated
$^1/_2$ pound mushrooms, sliced
12   ounces spaghetti
3-4 cups cooked turkey breasts,
     cut in $^1/_2$ cubes

Melt 3 tablespoons of butter. Mix in flour and cook, stirring until bubbly. Remove pan from heat and stir in broth, half-and-half and wine. Return to heat and cook stirring until sauce is smooth and thickened. Stir in Parmesan cheese. Measure out 1 cup of sauce and reserve both portions. Melt remaining butter in sauté pan. Add mushrooms and cook, stirring until juices evaporate and mushrooms are lightly browned. Cook and drain spaghetti. Combine cooked spaghetti with large portion of sauce, mushrooms (save a few for garnish) and turkey. Mix and season to taste. Turn into a greased casserole dish. Spoon 1 cup of reserved sauce evenly over the surface and top with reserved mushrooms. Bake at 375 degrees for 45 minutes (one hour if refrigerated).

Barbeque Turkey Breast

MARINADE:

4   garlic cloves, minced

2   tablespoons fresh ginger, peeled and minced

1 $^1/_2$ tablespoons poppy seeds

2   scallions, minced

1 $^1/_2$ cups reduced-sodium soy sauce

$^1/_4$ cup olive oil

2   tablespoons rice wine vinegar

juice of 3 lemons

$^1/_2$ teaspoon pepper, freshly ground

4   pounds boneless turkey breast with the skin on

GLAZE:

$^1/_2$ cup apricot preserves

$^1/_2$ cup Dijon mustard

1   teaspoon fresh ginger, peeled and minced

To make marinade: Whisk together all the marinade ingredients in a large bowl. Add the turkey, turn to coat with marinade. Cover and let marinate in the refrigerator, overnight.

To make glaze: Heat the ingredients for the glaze in a saucepan over moderately low heat until the apricot preserves are melted. Keep it warm. Remove the turkey from the marinade and pat it dry. Arrange it, skin side down, on a rack set 6-inches from the glowing coals and grill it for 15-20 minutes. Turn it over and grill it for an additional 10-15 minutes. Grill each side for another 5 minutes after brushing it with the warm glaze. (Check to make sure the turkey is just cooked through; if it isn't, grill it an additional 5 minutes.) Let the turkey breast stand for 10 minutes before carving.

Turkey Tamale Casserole

1 onion, chopped
1 red bell pepper, chopped
2 small zucchini, halved lengthwise and sliced
1$\frac{1}{2}$-2 cups cooked turkey or chicken, cubed
1 cup frozen corn kernels
1 can hominy, drained
1 can green enchilada sauce
1 small can black olives, sliced
1$\frac{1}{4}$ cups corn meal
1 cup water
$\frac{3}{4}$ cup milk
$\frac{1}{2}$ teaspoon salt
$\frac{2}{3}$ cup Cheddar or Monterey Jack cheese, grated

Preheat oven to 375 degrees. In a pot, cook onions, pepper and zucchini over medium heat until soft. Add turkey, corn, hominy, enchilada sauce and olives. Pour into a greased 9X13-inch casserole. Top with prepared cornmeal mixture. Sprinkle with cheese. Bake for 30-35 minutes.

To make cornmeal mixture: In a saucepan, combine cornmeal, water, milk and salt. Cook over medium-high heat, stirring frequently, for 5-7 minutes or until thickened.

Mom's Best Pot Roast

1 chuck roast or 7-bone roast (2-4 pounds)
1$\frac{1}{2}$ teaspoons seasoning salt
$\frac{1}{4}$ teaspoon garlic powder
$\frac{1}{4}$ teaspoon onion powder
$\frac{1}{2}$ teaspoon pepper
1 tablespoon flour
2 tablespoons vegetable oil
1 tablespoon Worcestershire sauce
$\frac{1}{4}$ cup soy sauce
3 cups water
$\frac{1}{2}$ cup flour
1 cup water

Heat oil in large heavy skillet, electric or ovenproof with a lid. Mix salt, pepper, onion and garlic powder and season both sides of the roast. Press flour into the roast. Slightly brown roast in oil on both sides. Sprinkle Worcestershire sauce and soy sauce over roast being careful not to burn yourself with the steam. Pour 3 cups water around roast and cover with a tight lid. Bake at 300 degrees for 3 hours or 250 degrees for 4 hours.

Blend flour and water until smooth to thicken drippings. Remove roast to a plate. Thicken drippings to desired consistency and correct any seasonings. If too strong, add additional water. Place roast back into gravy and hold until serving.

Note: If using electric skillet, turn heat to low. You may have to add additional water as the roast cooks for 3-4 hours.

Servings: 6-8

French Dip Sandwiches

1 (3 pound) sirloin tip roast
1 package Good Seasons® Zesty Italian Salad Dressing Mix
1 package au jus (Schilling® Natural Style)
1 (10 ounce) can beef broth
1 ¼ cups of water
French bread or hoagie buns

Brown roast on all sides in fry pan. Remove and place in crock-pot. Cover with all other ingredients. Cook for 8 hours on medium setting. Slice and serve on French bread or hoagie buns.

Stuffed Tuscany Tenderloin

2 tablespoons olive oil
1 medium onion, peeled and minced
½ pound fresh spinach, rinsed, stemmed and chopped
½ teaspoon salt
½ teaspoon black pepper, freshly ground
¼ cup Parmesan cheese, freshly grated
¼ cup oil-packed sun-dried tomatoes, finely chopped
1 (3-4 pound) beef tenderloin, cut from center of tenderloin
1 beef bouillon cube
¼ cup dry sherry
1 ½ cups water
fresh parsley sprigs

Preheat oven to 425 degrees. In large skillet, heat oil over medium heat. Add onion and cook until tender and golden, stirring occasionally. Add spinach, salt and pepper. Cook just until spinach wilts, stirring constantly, about 1 minute. Remove from heat and stir in Parmesan and sun-dried tomatoes. Make a lengthwise cut along the center of the tenderloin, cutting almost in half, but not all of the way through. Lay open, spread with spinach mixture and fold to enclose filling. Tie securely with string. Place cut-side up on rack in roasting pan. Cover stuffing with foil to prevent drying out. Cook 35-40 minutes, or to desired doneness.

Place on cutting board and cover with foil to keep warm. Remove rack from roasting pan. Skim and discard fat from drippings, add bouillon cube, sherry and water. Heat to boiling at medium-high, constantly stirring to loosen brown bits. Remove from heat. Slice tenderloin 1-inch thick and arrange on a warmed platter.

Garnish with parsley sprigs and serve with reserved sauce.

Servings: 8-10

Pot Roast with Bourbon

3-4 pound chuck roast
1   tablespoon dried oregano
1   tablespoon dried basil
6   slices bacon
1   cup bourbon

Preheat oven to 350 degrees. Cut 6 slits about 1-inch deep into the top of the roast. Combine herbs in bowl and add bacon. Roll up the bacon and stuff 1 slice in each slit. Pour bourbon over the meat, cover and roast for about 2 hours.

Barbeque Beef Brisket Sandwiches

4   pounds beef tri-tip
deli rolls

DRY RUB:
$1^1/_2$ teaspoons salt
$1^1/_2$ teaspoons pepper
2   tablespoons chili powder
2   teaspoons or 2 whole bay leaves
2   tablespoons liquid smoke

SAUCE:
3   tablespoons brown sugar
14 ounces ketchup
$^3/_4$ cup water
2   tablespoons liquid smoke
4   tablespoons Worcestershire sauce
3   teaspoons dry mustard
2   teaspoons mustard seed
6   tablespoons butter
cayenne pepper to taste
salt and pepper to taste

Mix dry rub ingredients. Rub on meat. Cook 10-12 hours at 250 degrees. After 2 hours, start shredding the cooking meat. Combine sauce ingredients and bring to boil. Reduce heat and let simmer for 10 minutes. Spread sauce over shredded meat. Let sit for 10 minutes for flavor of sauce to be absorbed by the brisket. Serve on deli rolls.

Fancy Fajitas

1/2 cup vegetable oil

3 tablespoons lemon juice

1 tablespoon wine vinegar

1/2 teaspoon garlic salt

1/2 teaspoon whole thyme

1/2 teaspoon chili powder

1 teaspoon whole oregano

1 medium onion, minced

2 pounds tenderloin or sirloin

10 (8-inch) flour tortillas

ACCOMPANIMENTS:

guacamole

sour cream

tomatoes

salsa

Monterey Jack cheese, grated

Combine oil, lemon juice, vinegar, garlic salt, thyme, chili powder, oregano and onion. Pour into a large resealable bag; add meat and marinate for 8-12 hours. Drain well. Grill tenderloin over hot grill, 7-8 minutes or until done. Slice meat into thin strips. Serve with warm tortillas.

To warm tortillas: Wrap a stack in foil. Heat in a 325 degree oven for 15 minutes.

Serve with accompaniments.

Weber State
UNIVERSITY

Founded in 1889, WSU is one of the West's finest undergraduate universities. Tour the art gallery or natural history museum. Watch a star show at the planetarium. A member of the Big Sky Athletic Conference, the Wildcats have been nationally ranked in men's basketball. The Ice Sheet, site of the 2002 Winter Games curling competition is also on campus.

Steak au Poivre

STEAK:

3   tablespoons black peppercorns

4   (6 ounce) beef filets,
     approximately 1¼-inch thick

2   tablespoons butter

1   tablespoon vegetable oil

SAUCE:

⅓   cup cognac

1   cup beef stock

½   cup heavy cream

salt to taste

To make steak: Wrap peppercorns in a clean dish towel and crush, either by pressing firmly with the bottom of a heavy skillet or by tapping gently with a mallet. (Peppercorns should be cracked, not ground.) Transfer pepper to a plate, then roll filets in it so that they are evenly coated. Season on both sides with salt.

Heat butter and oil in a large skillet over medium-high heat. Add filets and cook until well browned, about 4 minutes per side for medium rare. Transfer steaks to 4 warmed plates. Cover loosely with foil to keep warm while you prepare the sauce.

To make sauce: Add cognac to hot pan, then carefully ignite with a long-handled match. (Keep lid handy so flame can be extinguished if necessary.) Allow alcohol to burn off, about 1 minute, then add stock. Cook until reduced by half, about 4 minutes. Add cream and cook, stirring occasionally, until thick, 3-5 minutes. Season with salt and pour over steaks.

Barbeque Pork & Beef

1½   pounds beef stew meat

1½   pounds pork cubes

2   cups onions, chopped

½   cup brown sugar

⅛   cup chili powder

2   teaspoons Worcestershire

1   (6 ounce) can tomato paste

¼   cup cider vinegar

2   teaspoons salt

1   teaspoon dry mustard

Combine all ingredients, toss with meat. Add to crockpot. Cover and cook on high for 6½ hours. With wire whisk, stir mixture until meat is shredded.

Serve on French rolls.

Slow-Roasted Pork with Shallots, Apples & Cider

1   (3 pound) pork loin roast,
    boned and tied

Salt and pepper

15 whole shallots

3   apples, peeled, cored and
    quartered

2   cups apple cider

$^1/_4$ cup Dijon mustard

$^1/_3$ cup heavy cream

Preheat oven to 450 degrees. Place the pork in a roasting pan, generously season with salt and pepper. Place in the oven and roast for 20 minutes and then lower the heat to 325 degrees. Add the shallots, apples and cider. Roast for 2 hours or until the meat is tender.

Remove the meat from the pan, place on serving platter and scatter the shallots and apples around it.

Skim the excess fat from the liquid in the roasting pan. Add $^1/_2$ cup of water, then reduce over high heat by half. Stir in mustard and cream.

Pour some of the sauce over the roast and serve the rest on the side.

Serve warm or at room temperature.

Serves: 8

Pork Chops and Sliced Apples

6   pork chops
2$\frac{1}{2}$ cups sliced apples
2   tablespoons flour
2   tablespoons brown sugar
$\frac{1}{4}$ teaspoon salt
$\frac{1}{2}$ teaspoon cinnamon
$\frac{1}{3}$ cup boiling water

Brown pork chops on all sides and place in ovenproof baking dish. Combine all ingredients (except for water) and pour over chops. Then pour boiling water over top. Cover and bake at 300 degrees for 2 hours.

Kids love this recipe.

Southwestern Pork

3   pounds pork, cubed
3   tablespoons vegetable oil
1   tablespoon white vinegar
1$\frac{1}{2}$ teaspoons salt or to taste
1   large onion, finely chopped
1   green bell pepper, finely chopped
1   red bell pepper, finely chopped
1   jalapeño, seeds removed, finely chopped
4   cloves garlic, minced
1   small can diced green chilies
$\frac{1}{2}$ teaspoon ground oregano
$\frac{1}{2}$ teaspoon ground cumin
$\frac{1}{4}$ - $\frac{1}{2}$ cup fresh cilantro, chopped
cornstarch

ACCOMPANIMENTS:
flour tortillas
sour cream
Cheddar cheese, grated
lime

Brown pork in oil. Add vinegar and salt. Then add all chopped vegetables (onion -- garlic). Add green chilies and spices. Stir well. Bake at 225 degrees for 4-6 hours.

Before serving, thicken the pork mixture to desired thickness with cornstarch mixed in water. This will make it easier to wrap in a tortilla.

Stir in fresh cilantro at time of serving.

Serve with accompaniments.

Pork Chops in Balsamic Cherry Sauce

2   (5 ounce) boneless pork chops
    (each about 1-inch thick)
$^1/_3$ cup bottled balsamic
    vinaigrette
1   tablespoon butter
1   large shallot, thinly sliced
$^1/_3$ cup canned low-salt chicken
    broth
$^1/_4$ cup dried Bing (sweet) or tart
    cherries (about $1^1/_2$ ounces)
salt and pepper to taste

Place pork and vinaigrette in pie dish; turn to coat. Let stand 10 minutes. Melt butter in heavy medium skillet. Using tongs, lift pork from marinade; shake off excess. Transfer pork to skillet, reserving marinade in dish. Sprinkle pork with pepper. Sauté until brown, about 3 minutes per side. Transfer pork to plate. Add shallot to skillet; stir until softened, about one minute. Add broth, cherries and reserved marinade; bring to boil, scraping up browned bits. Return pork to skillet. Simmer until pork is cooked through, cherries are tender and sauce is slightly reduced, about 2 minutes per side. Season with salt and pepper. Transfer pork to plates; top with sauce.

Servings: 2

Golden Glow Pork Chops

5-6 pork chops
$^1/_4$ cup brown sugar
$^1/_2$ teaspoon ground cinnamon
$^1/_4$ teaspoon ground cloves
1   (8 ounce) can tomato sauce
$^1/_4$ cup apple cider vinegar
1   (29 ounce) can cling peach
    halves, syrup reserved
salt and pepper to taste

Lightly brown pork chops on both sides in large skillet or roasting pan. Pour off excess fat. Combine sugar, cinnamon, ground cloves, tomato sauce, vinegar and $^1/_4$ cup of syrup from peaches. Sprinkle chops with salt and pepper. Arrange chops in slow cooking pot. Place drained peach halves on top. Pour tomato mixture over the top. Cover and cook on low for 4-6 hours.

Shish Kabob Marinade

1   cup soy sauce
¹/₂ cup brown sugar
¹/₂ cup vinegar
¹/₂ cup pineapple juice
2   teaspoons salt
¹/₂ teaspoon garlic powder

Mix all ingredients and bring to a boil. Let cool. Marinate beef in mixture for at least 4 hours in refrigerator.

Leg of Lamb

1   medium leg of spring lamb
    (with the chine bone broken)
garlic salt to taste
4   (16 ounce) cans of small
    white potatoes, drained
mint jelly

Preheat oven to 350 degrees. Clean all visible fat and fell (looks like skin) from the lamb. Generously pour garlic salt over lamb leg. Place in oven on a pan large enough to add in potatoes and cook 20 minutes per pound of lamb. Halfway through cooking, add in potatoes stirring occasionally. Let stand 15 minutes before serving. Serve with mint jelly.

Lamb Cola

5   pound leg of lamb
1   tablespoon course sea salt
10 cloves of garlic
1   (12 ounce) can of cola, not
    diet
1   jar of jalapeño jelly
pepper to taste

Preheat oven to 400 degrees. Rub the lamb with salt and pepper. Cut slits in the fat and insert one clove of garlic in each slit. Pour the can of cola over the lamb, cover with tin foil and bake for 25 minutes. Reduce heat to 325 degrees, uncover the lamb and continue cooking for about one hour, basting often. Heat the jelly in a saucepan and serve as an accompaniment to the lamb.

Chopped Braised Leeks & Salmon

1½ pound skimmed salmon fillet
4   pounds whole leeks
3   tablespoons butter
½   cup celery, chopped
½   cup chicken broth
½   cup chives, chopped
salt and freshly ground pepper to
    taste

ALTERNATIVE FISH:

halibut
cod
bass
snapper

GARNISH:

chives
2   tablespoons salmon caviar

ACCOMPANIMENT:

carrots

The leeks and salmon braise together in a 1-pan, no-fuss meal. Chopped leeks may be prepared a day ahead and final cooking only takes a few minutes. Garnish with chopped chives and salt and pepper to taste.

Remove any bones in the salmon, cut the fillet into 4 equal portions, cover and refrigerate.

Remove any withered outer leaves of the leeks and cut off and discard the green upper leaves down to the point where the dark green begins to pale. Quarter the leeks lengthwise from the top down to within 1½-inches from the base and gently fan out the leaves so that any soil or grit on the leaves is easy to remove. Fill the sink or deep pan with lukewarm water and plunge the leeks up and down in the water until they are clean, then pat them dry. To chop, cut across the leeks in ½-inch slices. (Approximately 8 cups chopped leeks.)

In a large frying pan, melt the butter, add celery and chopped leeks and stir to coat the vegetables with butter. Pour in the chicken broth and cook for 3-4 minutes, or until the vegetables are just wilted. Season with salt and freshly ground pepper to taste. (To serve as a vegetable without the fish, continue to cook for 2-3 minutes more, covered, stirring occasionally.)

Place the salmon fillets on the top of the chopped, braised leeks, cover, reduce the heat and braise gently for 10 minutes, regulating the heat so that the leeks don't brown. Remove the braised leeks to warm serving plates, top each bed of leeks with a piece of salmon. Sprinkle chopped chives over the leeks and salmon and garnish with salmon caviar (optional).

Accompaniment: Braised baby carrots or carrot logs make an ideal side dish and add a complementary color.

Bacon, Scallops & Kielbasa Sausage

½ pound bacon, cut in ½-inch pieces
1 onion, chopped
2 cloves garlic, minced
1 teaspoon thyme
1 teaspoon pepper
1 teaspoon oregano
⅓ cup red wine
2 tablespoons soy sauce
2 cubes beef bouillon base
6 ounces fresh (or frozen) spinach, chopped
8 ounces sea scallops
2 diced tomatoes
6 ounces kielbasa sausage, chopped
1 pound bag farfalle (bow-tie) pasta
Parmesan cheese, grated
garlic toast

Fry bacon until crispy, remove the bacon and reserve the grease. Discard ½ of the grease and put the onions and garlic in the pan with the remaining grease. Cook over medium-high heat for 10 minutes. Add spices and cook for another 10 minutes. Onions should start to caramelize. Add wine and cook for 5 minutes. Add soy sauce and beef cubes; cook another 5 minutes. Add scallops, sausage, tomatoes and spinach; cook for 5 minutes. Add pasta cooked al denté and toss well. Serve on a big plate with garlic toast and Parmesan cheese.

Servings: 4

Bourbon-Basted Salmon

1½ pound salmon fillet

MARINADE:

¼ cup brown sugar
3 tablespoons bourbon
3 tablespoons green onions, chopped
2 tablespoons soy sauce
2 tablespoons vegetable oil

Place salmon, skin side down, in a shallow baking dish. Remove all bones. In a small bowl, combine all marinade ingredients. Pour over salmon and marinate in refrigerator at least 1 hour.

Brush the insides of the fish grilling basket or aluminum foil with vegetable oil. Remove salmon from marinade; reserve marinade. Place salmon in basket and close securely. Grill salmon in basket over hot coals, turning once, until opaque throughout, about 7 minutes per side. Baste with reserved marinade during cooking. Serve hot or cold.

Pan-Seared Tuna with Ginger, Miso & Cilantro Sauce

MARINADE:

2 tablespoons fresh lemon juice

2 tablespoons oriental sesame oil

2 tablespoons soy sauce

1 teaspoon ground black pepper

6 (5 ounce) ahi tuna steaks
   (about 1-1$\frac{1}{4}$-inches thick)

non-stick vegetable oil spray

ginger, miso and cilantro sauce

fresh cilantro sprigs

SAUCE:

1$\frac{1}{2}$ teaspoons oriental sesame oil

$\frac{1}{2}$ cup shallots, minced

1 tablespoon fresh ginger,
   minced and peeled

1 cup canned low-salt chicken
   broth

$\frac{1}{4}$ cup frozen orange juice
   concentrate, thawed

3 tablespoons rice vinegar

2 tablespoons yellow miso
   (fermented soybean paste*) or
   soy sauce

2 tablespoons fresh cilantro,
   chopped

* Available at Japanese markets
   and specialty foods stores and
   in the Asian foods sections of
   some supermarkets.

To make marinade: Whisk lemon juice, sesame oil, soy sauce and pepper in small bowl to blend. Place tuna steaks in a 9x13-inch glass-baking dish. Pour marinade over tuna steaks; turn to coat. Cover and refrigerate 3 hours, turning occasionally.

Remove tuna from marinade. Spray large non-stick skillet with vegetable oil spray. Heat skillet over high heat. Add 3 tuna steaks to skillet and cook about 3 minutes per side for medium-rare. Transfer tuna steaks to plate. Tent with aluminum foil to keep warm. Repeat with remaining 3 tuna steaks.

Transfer tuna steaks to plates. Spoon ginger, miso and cilantro sauce atop tuna. Garnish with cilantro and serve.

To make sauce: Heat oil in heavy small saucepan over medium-high heat. Add shallots and ginger and sauté 2 minutes. Add broth, orange juice concentrate and vinegar. Boil until mixture is reduced to $\frac{3}{4}$ cup, about 6 minutes. (Can be made 1 day ahead. Cover and chill. Return to boil before continuing.) Stir in miso and cilantro. Simmer 1 minute. Season with salt and pepper.

Suggestion: Using a marinade like this one is a good way to add flavor and richness to food without adding too many calories. Serve the tuna with steamed rice and offer Japanese beer or iced jasmine tea to drink.

Servings: 6

Sautéed Shrimp with Gorgonzola Sauce

16   large uncooked shrimp,
     peeled and deveined, tails
     intact

all-purpose flour for dredging

1   tablespoon butter
2   tablespoons brandy
$^1/_3$ cup whipping cream
$^1/_3$ cup Gorgonzola cheese,
     crumbled
$^1/_3$ cup Parmesan cheese, grated
1$^1/_2$ teaspoon minced fresh
     marjoram or $^1/_2$ teaspoon
     dried and crumbled

Dredge shrimp with flour, shake off excess. Melt butter in heavy large skillet over high heat. Add shrimp and sauté 1 minute. Add brandy and cook 30 seconds. Add cream, Gorgonzola, Parmesan and marjoram. Boil until shrimp are cooked through and sauce thickens, stirring frequently and turning shrimp with tongs, about 3 minutes. Divide shrimp between plates and spoon sauce over the top.

Asian Salmon

2   (8 ounce) salmon fillets
2   tablespoons brown sugar
2   tablespoons sesame oil
$^1/_4$ cup soy sauce

juice of one lemon

2   garlic cloves, minced
1   jalapeño pepper, seeded and
     finely chopped

Mix all ingredients. Marinate salmon 1 hour, turning after 30 minutes. Grill approximately 5 minutes or broil 8-10 minutes per inch of thickness.

Shrimp & Squash Risotto

2　cups butternut squash, peeled and diced

3¹/₂-4 cups fat free low sodium chicken or vegetable broth

2　tablespoons olive oil or butter, divided

1　pound large shrimp, peeled and deveined

3　cloves garlic, minced

¹/₄　teaspoon crushed red pepper flakes

1　large onion, chopped

1　cup Arborio rice

¹/₄　cup chopped fresh dill, chives, or Italian parsley

salt to taste

Preparation: 30 minutes Cooking: 20 minutes

In a medium-size saucepan, bring broth to a simmer. Adjust heat to maintain a gentle simmer. Heat 1 tablespoon of the oil in a large deep skillet or sauté pan over medium-high heat. Add shrimp, garlic and pepper flakes; sauté 3 minutes or until shrimp are opaque. Transfer to a bowl; set aside.

Heat remaining oil in pan. Add squash and onion; sauté 3 minutes. Add rice; sauté 1 minute.

Using a large ladle, transfer about 1 cup broth to the rice mixture. Cook, stirring occasionally, until most of liquid is absorbed. Continue adding broth 1 ladle full at a time, stirring occasionally until rice is slightly firm to the bite and squash is tender, about 20 minutes, keeping at a constant simmer. Stir in reserved shrimp mixture and salt to taste; heat through. Ladle into shallow bowls; top with herbs.

Servings: 4

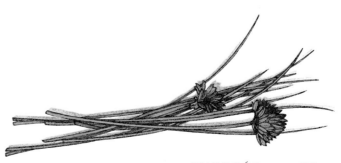

Crab Giovanni

2 cups onions, chopped
$^1/_2$ pound fresh mushrooms, sliced
2 cloves garlic, minced or mashed
$^1/_2$ cup ($^1/_4$ pound) butter or margarine, melted
$^1/_2$ pound spaghetti or vermicelli, cooked
2-3 cups crabmeat
$^1/_2$ cup sliced stuffed green olives
$^1/_2$ pound shredded sharp Cheddar cheese, grated
$^1/_2$ cup sour cream
1 (1 pound, 12 ounce) large can tomatoes, broken in pieces
1 $^1/_2$ teaspoons salt
$^1/_2$ teaspoon basil

Easy and may be refrigerated one or 2 days before baking.

In a large frying pan, slowly sauté the onions, mushrooms and garlic in butter until tender. Combine with remaining ingredients, stirring until well mixed. Pour mixture into greased 3-quart casserole or baking dish and bake, uncovered, at 350 degrees for 35-45 minutes, or until hot and bubbly. (If the dish has been refrigerated, allow about 1 hour baking time).

Servings: 8-10

Hot Crab Sandwiches

1 (6 ounce) can crabmeat or equivalent fresh crab
6-8 ounce cream cheese, softened
$^1/_4$ cup sharp Cheddar cheese (or more), grated
1 teaspoon ground horseradish
$^1/_4$ teaspoon Tabasco® sauce
1 teaspoon prepared mustard
$^1/_4$ teaspoon garlic salt
mayonnaise for thickening
4 hamburger buns, split, or Triscuit® crackers

Mix all ingredients together, add small amount of mayonnaise to make it spreadable. Spread on the buns or crackers and broil until lightly browned.

Shrimp Casserole

2¹/₂ pounds large shrimp, shelled and deveined

1 tablespoon lemon juice

3 tablespoons vegetable oil

³/₄ cup rice or 1 cup precooked rice

2 tablespoons butter

¹/₄ cup green bell pepper, minced

¹/₄ cup onion, minced

1 teaspoon salt

¹/₈ teaspoon black pepper

dash cayenne pepper

1 (10¹/₄ ounce) can condensed tomato soup, undiluted

1 cup heavy cream

1 cup sherry

³/₄ cup blanched almonds, slivered

Early on in the day: Cook shrimp in boiling, salted water for 5 minutes; drain. Place in 2-quart casserole dish, (set aside 8 shapely shrimp for garnish.) Sprinkle with lemon juice and vegetable oil. Meanwhile, cook rice as label directs; drain. Refrigerate for about an hour before serving.

Preheat oven to 350 degrees. Add butter to skillet, sauté green bell pepper and onion for 5 minutes. Add rice, salt, black pepper, cayenne pepper, soup, cream, sherry and ¹/₂ cup almonds. Pour mixture over shrimp in casserole dish. Toss well.

Bake uncovered 35 minutes. Top with 8 reserved shrimp and remaining almonds. Bake 20 minutes longer, or until mixture is bubbly and shrimp is slightly browned.

Servings: 6-8

Accompaniment: Serve with a crispy salad and you have got an easy meal.

Curried Tuna Sandwich

1 can tuna, drained

¹/₃ - ¹/₂ cup water chestnuts, sliced

1 teaspoon Worcestershire sauce

1 teaspoon curry powder

3 green onions, minced

mayonnaise

English muffins

Stir ingredients together with enough mayonnaise to moisten the mixture for spreading on the English muffins and then broil sandwiches until golden.

Notes:

Painting by: Liz Pierce

J unior League of Ogden (JLO) has a history of commitment to the support and welfare of women and children. The Weber/Morgan Children's Justice Center (CJC), shown above in its previous home, provides a safe haven for child victims of crime. Junior League of Ogden has helped support the CJC through donations as well as through volunteer hours spent refurbishing rooms in the building. As an advocate for children's issues, Junior League of Ogden has also been a supporter of the Marshall White Center located in the heart of Ogden. Each fall, JLO serves more than one thousand children in a two-day health screening program for underinsured children. Named the Children's Health Connection, this project is made possible through a partnership with McKay Dee Hospital and other community partners.

Painting by: Julie Lewis

CHILDREN'S RECIPES

Dinner in a Pumpkin

1   small to medium pumpkin
1   onion, chopped
2   tablespoons vegetable oil
1½-2 pounds ground beef
2   tablespoons soy sauce
2   tablespoons brown sugar
1   (4 ounce) can, sliced
     mushrooms, drained
1   (10¾ ounce) can cream of
     chicken soup
1½ cups rice, cooked
1   (8 ounce) can sliced water
     chestnuts, drained

Cut off the top of the pumpkin and thoroughly clean out the seeds and pulp. Paint an appropriate face on the front with a permanent marker. Preheat oven to 350 degrees. In a large skillet, sauté onions in oil until tender. Add meat and brown. Drain drippings, add soy sauce, brown sugar, mushrooms and soup. Simmer 10 minutes, stirring occasionally. Add cooked rice and water chestnuts. Spoon mixture into the cleaned pumpkin shell. Replace top and place entire pumpkin with filling on a baking sheet. Bake 1 hour or until inside of pumpkin is tender. Cooking time may vary up to 2 hours, depending on size of pumpkin. Place entire pumpkin on serving platter, remove lid and serve mixture plus meat of the pumpkin.

Mini-Pizzas

English muffins (plain, sourdough,
     or whole wheat)
jar of pizza sauce
mozzarella cheese, shredded
favorite pizza meats, fruits or
     veggies (Canadian bacon,
     pepperoni, pineapple, green
     peppers, olives, etc.)

Heat oven to 350 degrees. Line a cookie or jelly roll pan with foil. Make each pizza (fun for the kids to do) by spreading sauce on an English muffin, then adding cheese and toppings as desired. Place pizzas on pan. Bake until cheese is melted.

To serve: Each pizza can be served whole or sliced as you would a regular-sized pizza.

Crunchy Oven Baked Nuggets

3 cups cornflakes
$^1/_2$ teaspoon poultry seasoning
$^1/_4$ teaspoon pepper
$^1/_4$ teaspoon salt
1 large egg
2 tablespoons milk
$^1/_4$ teaspoon Tabasco® sauce
1 pound chicken tenders, cut into nugget shape

Heat oven to 375 degrees. Place cornflakes in large resealable plastic bag. Lay bag on flat surface and crush cornflakes, using a rolling pin. Combine cornflakes, poultry seasoning, pepper and salt in shallow bowl. In separate bowl, whisk together egg, milk and Tabasco® sauce. Add several chicken nuggets at a time to egg mixture, coating well. Dredge and roll in cornflake mixture. Place on foil lined baking sheet. Generously spray chicken pieces on both sides with vegetable cooking spray. Bake nuggets for 15-18 minutes, or until cooked through. To reheat frozen nuggets, heat oven to 350 degrees. Place nuggets on baking sheet and bake 10-12 minutes.

Hedgehogs

lettuce
cottage cheese
canned pears or peaches
pretzel sticks, halved
whole cloves

For each hedgehog, place a lettuce leaf on a plate. Top with a dollop of cottage cheese. Place half of a canned peach or pear on the cottage cheese, smooth side up. Poke pretzel sticks all over peach or pear for "spikes" and poke 2 cloves on pointier side of peach or pear for eyes. Raisins can be used instead of cloves, but they don't stick as well.

Monkey Bread

3 tubes buttermilk biscuits, quartered
1 cup white sugar
2 teaspoons cinnamon
1 stick butter
1 cup brown sugar

Cut each biscuit into quarters. In a resealable bag combine white sugar and cinnamon. Add quartered biscuits and shake until covered. Arrange in a greased bundt pan. Melt butter and brown sugar and bring to a boil. Cook 1 minute. Pour over biscuits in bundt pan. Bake at 350 degrees for 30-35 minutes. Turn upside down on a plate.

CHILDREN'S
Treehouse Museum

Named one of the top 50 children's museums in the nation by Child Magazine, Treehouse Museum is the storybook place for children and families. This hands-on museum focuses on family literacy, children's literature and the arts. Treehouse offers dozens of beautiful and award-winning exhibits and daily programming for children, ages 2-12 and their grown-ups. Families can sit in Grandma Sofie's lap and share a story or play the Utah Challenge Game on the giant floor map of the State. Children can explore medieval times in the Days of the Knights Exhibit, make music on hand-made marimbas and drums in the Pick Up a Stick and Play Exhibit, attend school in the One Room Schoolhouse Exhibit and much more. With Art and Computer Gardens, a Castle Theater and a Party Room, Treehouse is the magical museum where children really do step into a story.

Dinosaur Claws

1 can of refrigerator biscuits
margarine, melted
cinnamon sugar
almond slivers

Bake the biscuits according to package directions, usually about 8-10 minutes. Brush each biscuit with melted margarine and sprinkle biscuits with cinnamon sugar. While the biscuit is still warm, carefully insert 5 almond slivers around the edge of the biscuit so it looks like the claws of a dinosaur.

With a permanent marker, draw dinosaur tracks on the edges of a clean square of cardboard. Serve the claws on the cardboard squares.

OGDEN ECCLES
Dinosaur Park

At the Ogden Eccles Dinosaur Park, you can wander through the Dinosaur Age, imagining the Earth when it was inhabited by the fierce predator Tyrannosaurus Rex or the gazelle-like Dryosaurus. Travel back in time and see life-size replicas of the creatures that lived two hundred million years ago. Located at the mouth of Ogden Canyon, these creatures are presented in a natural outdoor environment that includes sound. With just a little imagination you will believe you have truly traveled back in time to observe these creatures as they once existed. The new Elizabeth Dee Shaw Stewart Museum houses dramatic and hands-on exhibits of the latest dinosaur finds from Utah and around the world. From a life-size skeletal replica of a Tyrannosaurus Rex to a sand pit where junior paleontologists can excavate real dinosaur bones, the new museum offers something for everyone.

Spider Sandwiches

2 slices wheat sandwich bread
per person

sandwich spread, such as peanut
butter, tuna salad, soft cheese

$1/2$ can cheese curls or pretzel
sticks

raisins

Cut a circle from each bread slice with a $2^1/_2$-inch round cookie cutter. Divide the bread circles into 2 equal piles. Spread about 2 tablespoons of sandwich spread on all of the bread circles in one pile. Press 8 cheese curls or pretzel sticks in the sandwich spread half way around each circle to make the legs of the spider. Place the remaining bread circle on top of the sandwich spread-coated circles. Using a finger, poke 2 small indentations on top of each sandwich. Push 1 raisin into each indentation to make spider eyes.

Draw a spider web with a permanent black marker on the edges of a paper plate. Place 1 spider sandwich on each plate and serve for a silly lunch.

Flintstone Dip

2 cups mayonnaise

2 cups sour cream

2 teaspoons Beau Monde
Seasoning

2 teaspoons dry parsley

1 tablespoon dry onion

2 (2 ounce) packages dried beef,
chopped

Combine all ingredients. Refrigerate for 2 hours or more before serving. Serve with crackers or Frito® chips.

Crispy Treats

½ cup butter or margarine
2 cups miniature marshmallows
   or about 40 large ones
¼ cup creamy peanut butter
   (optional)
5 cups puffed crispy rice cereal

OPTIONAL ICING:
1 cup butterscotch chips
1 cup chocolate chips

Melt butter in microwave. Add marshmallows and microwave about 3 minutes until puffed. Stir until smooth. Stir in peanut butter, if desired. Add cereal and quickly mix. Press into a greased 9x13-inch pan, using a piece of waxed paper to keep mixture from sticking to your hands. Cut into squares.

In microwave, melt butterscotch chips or milk chocolate chips. Spread over top of treats. Chill and cut into squares.

Muddy Bites

12 ounces milk chocolate chips
½   stick butter or margarine
1   cup creamy peanut butter
1   box Crispix® cereal
2   cups powdered sugar

Melt chocolate chips, butter, or margarine and peanut butter in a large bowl in microwave. Add cereal and gently mix to coat. Cool. Place sugar in a paper grocery bag and shake cereal mixture into bag to coat. Add more powdered sugar if necessary.

Potato Chip Cookies

1 cup white sugar
1 cup brown sugar
1 cup shortening
2 eggs
2 cups plus 2 tablespoons flour
1 teaspoon baking soda
2 cups regular flavored potato
   chips, crushed
1 teaspoon vanilla
1 (12 ounce) package
   butterscotch chips

Cream the sugars and shortening. Add eggs, flour, baking soda, potato chips and vanilla. Stir in bag of butterscotch chips. Drop by spoonfuls onto lightly greased cookie sheet. Bake at 375 degrees for 10 minutes. Do not over bake.

Monster Cookies

12 eggs
2 pounds brown sugar
4 cups white sugar
2 cups butter, softened
1 tablespoon vanilla
1 tablespoon light corn syrup
3 pounds peanut butter
8 teaspoon baking powder
1 box (2 pounds 10 ounce) quick oats
1 pound bag plain M&M's®
1 pound chocolate chips

Heat oven to 350 degrees. Beat eggs in a large bowl. Add sugars, butter, vanilla and corn syrup. Mix well. Stir in peanut butter, baking powder, quick oats, M&M's® and chocolate chips. Form into 3-inch balls to make monster-sized cookies. Bake for 12-15 minutes.

Cinnamon Ornaments

2 cups ground cinnamon
2 cups applesauce
Raffia ribbon or string

In a large mixing bowl, combine cinnamon and applesauce. Mix with hands to make dough. Adjust each ingredient to make a stiff dough. Form into a ball and with a rolling pin roll out to $1/4$-inch thick. Cut into shapes with your favorite cookie cutters. Use a straw to poke a hole in ornament for the ribbon or string to be tied on later. Transfer to baking sheet. Bake at 250 degrees for 25-30 minutes or until dried and hard consistency. Cool. Attach raffia ribbon or string to make finished ornament.

Magic Marshmallow Crescent Puffs

¹/₄ cup sugar

1 teaspoon cinnamon

2 (8 ounce) cans refrigerated crescent dinner rolls

16 large marshmallows

¹/₄ cup margarine or butter, melted

¹/₄ cup nuts, chopped if desired

GLAZE:

¹/₂ cup powdered sugar

2-3 teaspoons milk

¹/₂ teaspoon vanilla

Heat oven to 375 degrees. Combine sugar and cinnamon. Separate crescent dough into 16 triangles. Dip a marshmallow in melted margarine; roll in sugar-cinnamon mixture. Place marshmallow on shortest side of triangle. Fold corners over marshmallow and roll to opposite point, completely covering marshmallow and pinching edges of dough to seal. Dip in melted margarine and place margarine-side down in deep muffin cup. Repeat with remaining marshmallows. Place pan on foil or cookie sheet during baking to guard against spillage. Bake for 10-15 minutes or until golden brown. Immediately remove from pans. Combine glaze ingredients; drizzle over warm rolls. Sprinkle with nuts.

Servings: 16 rolls

Funny Face Snack

rice cakes

peanut butter or flavored cream cheese

fresh or canned fruit slices, raisins, dried fruit, vegetable slices, etc.

Spread peanut butter or cream cheese over rice cake. Use fruit or other food to decorate like a face. Can be made with peanut butter, banana and apple slices or try vegetable-herb cream cheese with broccoli, celery and carrot pieces.

Mud Pie Cake

1½ cups all-purpose flour
1   cup sugar
¼   cup unsweetened cocoa
      powder
1   teaspoon baking soda
½   teaspoon salt
⅓   cup cooking oil
1   tablespoon vinegar
1   teaspoon vanilla
1   cup water

In a 1 gallon heavy-duty resealable plastic bag, place the flour, sugar, cocoa powder, soda and salt. Close bag and seal. Shake to mix well. Put the flour mixture into an ungreased 8x8-inch baking pan.

Use a table fork to make a hole in the middle of the flour mixture. In a 1-cup glass-measuring cup, measure the oil. Add the vinegar and vanilla. Pour the oil mixture into the hole. In the same measuring cup, measure the water. Pour the water into the hole.

Use the fork to stir together all ingredients. Bake at 350 degrees for 35-40 minutes or until done in the middle. Remove from oven, let cool in the pan on a wire rack. Cut into 12 pieces.

If desired, top with a scoop of vanilla ice cream, chocolate syrup and a maraschino cherry.

Servings: 12

Caramel Marshmallows

½   can sweetened condensed milk
½   stick butter
1   package caramels
1   bag large marshmallows
puffed rice cereal or toasted
      coconut

Put milk, butter and caramels in microwave safe bowl. Cover with a paper towel and microwave until melted. Remove and stir well. Dip large marshmallows in caramel mixture, then roll in cereal or toasted coconut. Place on wax paper to cool.

Lemon Lights

grape juice
lemonade mix

Fill each compartment of an ice cube tray with grape juice and place in the freezer. Let freeze overnight. The next day, prepare lemonade in a pitcher. Remove the ice cubes from the freezer. Take the ice cubes out of the tray. Place several cubes in each glass. Pour lemonade over the ice cubes and serve.

While drinking, watch what happens to the colors in the lemonade.

Moo-Cow Milk Shake

vanilla ice cream
ice cream scoop
1 (2 cup) plastic jar with tight-fitting lid
spoon
chocolate syrup
milk
tall glass

Remove ice cream from freezer. Allow to sit on the counter at room temperature about 15 minutes or until soft enough to scoop. Scoop ice cream into the jar until half full.

Add desired amount of chocolate syrup to ice cream in the jar. Pour milk into the jar until it is about $^3/_4$ full. Mix with a spoon. (If you prefer a vanilla shake, leave out the chocolate syrup.)

Put the lid onto the jar and tighten. (A screw top jar works best because you can shake without spilling.) With adult help, shake hard until ice cream and milk are mixed, about 3 minutes. Remove the jar lid. Pour the milk shake into a glass.

Yields: 1 shake

Silly Putty

4 tablespoons powdered starch
¹/₂ cup water
washable liquid paint
1 cup Elmer's® glue

Put the powdered starch and water together in a bowl. Stir until the starch is dissolved. Add paint and glue to the mixture. Let the mixture sit for a few minutes. Stir together until it starts to set and then knead until pliable, but not sticky. Store in a plastic bag in the refrigerator.

Note: This is a chemical reaction, so you can not change any of the ingredients. If the silly putty is too sticky, you need more starch, about 1 teaspoon. It doesn't take very much more to make a difference. If the silly putty is too stiff, it is too hard to fix so start over.

Ooblick

2 parts water
1 part corn starch
liquid washable paint

Mix the water together with the corn starch. The mixture should set up and look like a solid, but when you grab a handful, it will become runny and drip out of your hand. If the mixture is too runny and will not form a solid ball then add more corn starch. If it is too hard, add a little more water. Add drops of washable paint to color.

Playdough

2 cups flour
¹/₂ cup salt
2 tablespoons alum
¹/₃ cup vegetable oil
2 cups boiling water
washable paint or Kool Aid® mix

OPTIONAL:
potpourri oil

Put flour, salt, alum, vegetable oil and washable paint in a bowl. Pour boiling water over and mix. Knead until mixture is the desired consistency. If it is too sticky, add more flour. Store in a resealable plastic bag or container in the refrigerator.

Kool Aid® adds color and a fun fruit scent. For a floral scent replace Kool Aid® with approximately 10 drops of potpourri oil (such as rose, gardenia, lavender or jasmine).

Frilly Bubbles

1   cup water
¹⁄₄   cup sugar
¹⁄₂   cup Joy® liquid detergent
1   tablespoon glycerin

Mix all ingredients together until the sugar dissolves. Let the mixture stand for 3-4 hours.

Note: Form pipe cleaners into various shapes to create wand for blowing bubbles.

Print Maker Bubbles

2   cups washable paint
1   cup water
¹⁄₂   cup liquid starch
1   cup liquid detergent

Mix all ingredients together. Place mixture in a tub then lightly dip one side of paper into the bubble mixture until you achieve the effect you want.

Great for making gift wrap paper.

Note: May substitute washable paint with desired amount of food coloring.

Puffy Paint

1 cup Elmer's® school glue
2 cups shaving cream (non-menthol)
tempera paint (desired amount)

In a large mixing bowl, pour in glue. Fold in the shaving cream and mix thoroughly. You may need to adjust ingredient quantities to get desired consistency. Use this mixture as you would any other kind of craft paint but to get a puffy texture. Makes cute snowman picture or other winter scenes. Do not attempt to store. Mix and use the paint as needed.

Salt Paint

$^2/_3$ cup salt
$^1/_2$ teaspoon washable paint
pinch of talcum powder or cornstarch

Mix ingredients thoroughly. Spread on a tray to dry. Pour into a large-hole salt shaker to use.

Sand Paint

1 cup sifted, clean, dry sand
2 tablespoons powdered tempera
watered down glue

Mix ingredients thoroughly. Pour into a large-hole salt shaker to use.

NOTE:
Empty talcum powder containers with shaker tops or salt shakers with large-hole shaker tops make good sand and salt paint containers.

SUGGESTIONS:
Salt or sand paint can be used by sketching a picture and then brushing watered glue on the picture and shaking the paint over the desired area. This works great when making 'beach pictures' or for a textured project, write the child's name in glue and sift the sand over the letters. After it dries, the child can feel his/her name for a tactile experience.

Use salt or sand paint to layer colors in a jar or bottle for a fun activity.

Notes:

Finishing Touches

DELICIOUS DESSERTS

Painting by: Scott Wallis

When the driving of the Golden Spike completed the Transcontinental Railroad in 1869, Ogden was named Junction City. Painting the landscape with their bright boxcars and colorful whistles, the trains and the goods they transported raised Ogden's Union Station to an important hub. Today, Union Station is home to the Utah State Railroad Museum as well as other museums, galleries, shops and a locally owned restaurant. The newest and most dramatic exhibit in Ogden's Union Station is a 1940's little yellow caboose located inside the station building.

Painting by: Terry C. Johnson

The walls are lime green. The floor is a weird mosaic. The advertising on the wall is vintage 1930's. The place is Farr's Ice Cream and you haven't seen Ogden at its best until you've been to Farr's. Family owned and operated in Ogden for four generations.

DELICIOUS DESSERTS

Never Fail Pie Crust

2 cups flour
1 teaspoon salt
1 cup shortening or $^2/_3$ cup lard (this is best)
1 tablespoon vinegar
8 tablespoons cold water

Mix together and chill the dough. Roll to fit pie tin. When cooking the crust, the edge should be covered by aluminum foil to prevent it from overcooking.

Suggestion: Use a small leaf cookie cutter and place leaves around the edge of the crust. This makes a beautiful presentation for Thanksgiving.

Yield: 2 (8-inch) shells

Strawberry Pie

CRUST:
3 tablespoons milk
$^2/_3$ cup salad oil
2 cups sifted flour
2 teaspoons sugar
$1^1/_4$ teaspoons salt

PIE FILLING:
$1^1/_2$ cups sugar
$^1/_4$ cup cornstarch
$1^1/_2$ cups water
1 (3 ounce) package of strawberry gelatin
fresh strawberries

To make crust: Beat milk and oil until cloudy; set aside. Mix dry ingredients. Then mix with milk and oil using mixer until crumbly. Push into place in pie plate. Bake at 400 degrees for 8-10 minutes. Cool before filling.

To make filling: Mix sugar, cornstarch and water in saucepan and boil until transparent. Add package of strawberry gelatin and boil until dissolved. Slice fresh strawberries and fill cooled crust. After above mixture has cooled a little, pour over strawberries and let set at least 2 hours in refrigerator.

Yield: 1 (8-inch) pie

Southern Pecan Pie

1   (8-inch) pie pastry shell,
    unbaked
1   cup light brown sugar, firmly
    packed
1/2 cup white sugar
1   tablespoon flour
2   eggs
2   tablespoons milk
1   teaspoon vanilla
1/2 cup butter, melted (do not
    substitute)
1   cup pecans, chopped
    whipped cream or ice cream for
    topping (optional)

Mix brown sugar, white sugar and flour. Add eggs, milk, vanilla and melted butter; beat well. Fold in pecans. Pour into unbaked pastry shell. Bake at 375 degrees for 40-50 minutes.

Serve slightly warm. Top servings with whipped cream or ice cream, if desired.

Timbermine's Mud Pie

2   cups crushed
    Oreo® cookies
2   tablespoons
    butter, melted
1   gallon mocha ice
    cream, softened
    hot fudge topping
    whipped cream
    maraschino cherries

In a 9x13-inch cake pan, mix crushed cookies and butter, press in bottom of pan. Pour softened ice cream on top of cookie mixture and place in freezer overnight. When firm, heat hot fudge topping until you can easily spread over the ice cream, cover completely. Return to freezer for 2 more hours. Before serving cut in 2x2-inch squares and top with whipped cream and maraschino cherry if desired.

Nestled at the mouth of Ogden Canyon and next to the Ogden River, sits the Timbermine Steakhouse. Upon entering the cozy restaurant, you are immediately transported back in time by its atmosphere of the mining and gold digging era.

Coconut Cream Pie

CRUST:

8 whole graham crackers
$1/4$ cup sugar
6 tablespoons butter, chilled and diced

FILLING:

1 cup plus 2 tablespoons sweetened flaked coconut
$2^1/4$ cups whole milk
$1^1/4$ teaspoons unflavored gelatin
6 tablespoons sugar
3 tablespoons cornstarch
1 large egg
2 large egg yolks
1 teaspoon vanilla
$1^1/2$ tablespoons unsalted butter
pinch of salt
$1/2$ cup chilled whipping cream

TOPPING:

$1^1/2$ cups chilled whipping cream
2 tablespoons powdered sugar
$1/4$ cup toasted coconut (reserved)

To make crust: Place graham crackers and sugar in food processor and chop until finely ground. Add diced butter and pulse several times. Press into 9-inch round pie plate. Bake 8-10 minutes until golden brown. Cool completely.

To make filling: Spread coconut on baking sheet. Bake at 350 degrees for 8 minutes. Stir to toast uniformly. Remove and set aside.

Sprinkle $1/4$ cup milk with gelatin. Let stand 15 minutes.

Place sugar and cornstarch in medium saucepan, gradually add $1/4$ cup milk. Whisk until smooth. Then add remaining milk, egg and egg yolks. Whisk until smooth.

Set aside $1/4$ cup coconut for topping. Then add balance of coconut to egg mixture. Add vanilla, butter and salt to that mixture. Heat until boiling-stirring constantly. Remove from heat, add gelatin mixture and stir until gelatin dissolves then transfer to large bowl. Place plastic wrap directly on filling and chill in refrigerator for 1 hour.

Beat whipping cream and powdered sugar until peaks form.

Pour chilled filling into cooled pie crust. Spread topping on pie. Sprinkle with toasted coconut. Refrigerate overnight.

Pumpkin Pie to Die For

2   (9-inch) pie pastry shells,
    unbaked
6   eggs
2¼ cup sugar
1   (29 ounce) can pumpkin
1   teaspoon vanilla
¼   teaspoon salt
2   teaspoons cinnamon, slightly
    rounded
⅓   teaspoon ground ginger
¼   teaspoon ground cloves
1   (12 ounce) can of evaporated
    milk
one can of water

Beat eggs until blended. Add sugar, a little at a time, on low speed. Stir in about ¼ of the can of pumpkin. Add vanilla and salt. Mix on low speed and set aside.

Mix together cinnamon, ginger, cloves and the remaining pumpkin. Add pumpkin and spice mixture to egg mixture on low until just mixed. Add evaporated milk plus one can of water.

Pour into prepared (9-inch) crusts. Bake at 350 degrees for 15 minutes then increase heat to 375 degrees for about 45 minutes.

Servings: 2 (9-inch) pies

Applesauce Cake

1½ cups applesauce
2   teaspoons baking soda
¾   cup sugar
¾   cup brown sugar
½   cup butter or margarine,
    softened
2   cups all-purpose flour
¼   teaspoon salt
½   teaspoon ground cloves
½   teaspoon ground nutmeg
½   teaspoon cinnamon
½   teaspoon allspice
1   cup raisins
1   cup dates, chopped
1   cup walnuts, chopped

Combine applesauce and baking soda in small bowl, set aside. Cream together sugars and butter or margarine in large bowl. Blend remaining ingredients together, add to large bowl. Stir in applesauce mixture. Blend well.

Pour into greased and floured 9x13-inch baking pan. Bake in preheated 300 degree oven for one hour. Cool and cut into squares to serve.

This delicious cake is unique because it does not contain eggs. It is good served with whipped cream or ice cream.

Union Grill ~ Caramel Bread Pudding

PUDDING

1¹/₂ cups sugar
4   eggs, beaten
1¹/₄ cups heavy whipping cream
1¹/₂ cups milk
¹/₄   pound melted butter
1¹/₄ pounds white bread (2 loaves),
       cubed
¹/₂   cup caramel sauce, below
non-stick cooking spray

CARAMEL SAUCE

¹/₂   cup white sugar
¹/₂   cup brown sugar
1   stick butter (¹/₂ cup)
1   cup syrup (corn or maple)
1¹/₃ cups heavy cream

To make pudding: Combine the sugar, eggs, heavy whipping cream, milk and melted butter in a bowl and mix together. Add the bread and fold it in. Put mixture in a 9x13-inch baking pan that is sprayed with non-stick pan spray. Pour the caramel sauce over the top and bake at 350 degrees for 30 minutes; check, rotate and bake up to 30 minutes more (or until golden brown).

To make sauce: Combine white sugar, brown sugar, butter and syrup in a pot and cook over medium-high heat until all ingredients liquefy. Caution: this sauce gets very hot so be careful. Remove from heat and add the cream.

Serve hot, in a bowl with vanilla ice cream and more caramel sauce.

Located at the base of Historic 25th Street in the Union Station, the Union Grill resides at the heart of Ogden's colorful history. With a railroad themed cosmopolitan atmosphere and an interesting menu, the Union Grill has become a local favorite dining spot.

Nut Pudding

3   eggs
1¹/₂ cups milk
1-1¹/₂ cups sugar
1   (3 ounce) envelope unflavored
       gelatin, dissolved in ¹/₄ cup
       cold water
1   teaspoon vanilla
1   cup walnuts, chopped
1¹/₂ cups heavy whipping cream

Beat eggs. Add milk and sugar; boil until slightly thick on very low heat, stirring constantly, as it will scorch easily. When mixture begins to thicken, take off burner and add gelatin and vanilla. Cool. Whip cream to form peaks. Fold nuts and whipped cream into the cooled mixture. Set overnight or for at least 6 hours in the refrigerator.

Chocolate Cola Cake

CAKE INGREDIENTS:

2   cups flour
2   cups sugar
1   stick butter or margarine
$^1/_2$ cup oil
3   tablespoons cocoa
1   cup cola
$1^1/_2$ cups mini-marshmallows
$^1/_2$ cup buttermilk
1   teaspoon baking soda
2   eggs
1   teaspoon vanilla

FROSTING INGREDIENTS:

1   box powdered sugar
1   stick butter or margarine
3   tablespoons cocoa
6   tablespoons cola
$^1/_2$ cup pecans or walnuts,
     chopped
1   teaspoon vanilla

To make cake: Mix flour and sugar in a large mixing bowl. In a pan, heat butter, oil, cocoa and cola until boiling, stirring occasionally. Add marshmallows and stir until smooth. Pour heated mixture over flour and sugar and mix well. Add buttermilk, baking soda, eggs and vanilla and beat for 2 minutes. Pour batter into a greased and floured 9x13-inch cake pan. Bake at 350 degrees for 30-40 minutes, or until toothpick comes out clean. Frost while warm.

To make frosting: Pour powdered sugar in a mixing bowl. In a pan, heat butter, cocoa and cola until boiling. Pour heated mixture over powdered sugar; beat well. Add nuts and vanilla; stir. Spread on cake while still warm.

Serve with ice cream.

Yield: 1 (9x13-inch) cake

Harvey Wallbanger Cake

1   package yellow cake mix
1   package vanilla instant
     pudding
1   cup cooking oil
4   eggs
$^1/_4$ cup vodka
$^1/_4$ cup Galliano
$^3/_4$ cup orange juice

Mix all ingredients together and beat 4 minutes. Pour batter into well greased bundt pan. Bake at 350 degrees for 45-50 minutes.

Yield: 1 cake

Red Velvet Cake

CAKE:

butter for greasing pans

2 cups all-purpose flour, plus extra for dusting pans

1 tablespoon unsweetened cocoa powder

1 teaspoon salt

1^1/$_2$ cups sugar

^{1}/$_2$ cup vegetable shortening

2 eggs

1 cup buttermilk

1 teaspoon vanilla extract

2 ounces red food coloring

1 teaspoon baking soda

1 teaspoon white vinegar

ICING:

4 egg yolks

^{2}/$_3$ cup sugar

^{1}/$_2$ cup whole milk

8 ounces unsalted butter, softened, plus additional if needed

1 tablespoon vanilla extract, bourbon or rum

GARNISH:

pecans, chopped or halved for decoration

To make Cake: Preheat oven to 350 degrees. Butter and then flour 2 (9-inch) round cake pans. Combine flour, cocoa and salt in a sifter and sift 3 times to thoroughly mix cocoa powder. Mix sugar and shortening with an electric mixer until blended. Beat in eggs, one at a time, mixing well after each addition. Beat another minute at medium speed. Alternately beat the flour mixture (in 4 parts) and the buttermilk (in 3 parts) into the sugar mixture. (Do not over beat.) Add the vanilla and food coloring and mix well to color evenly.

Dissolve baking soda in the vinegar and quickly fold it in. Pour half the batter into each prepared cake pan and bake until the cake top springs back when gently pressed, 20-25 minutes. Turn out layers onto wire racks and let cool.

To make icing: Place egg yolks in a large mixing bowl and gradually beat in sugar with a whisk or mixer. Beat until the mixture is a thick pale yellow and forms a ribbon when a spoonful is dropped on the surface. Heat milk to almost boiling and beat into the egg mixture by droplets. Pour into a heavy saucepan and cook over medium heat, stirring with a wooden spoon until mixture is thick enough to lightly coat the spoon (about 165 degrees on a candy thermometer). Immediately set the pan in a basin of cold water and beat until custard is barely tepid. Strain custard into another bowl and beat in softened butter by spoonfuls. Beat in flavoring. The icing should be smooth and thick. If it looks grainy or curdled, beat in additional softened butter, a teaspoonful at a time. Chill icing until cold but still spreadable.

Place one cake layer on a serving platter and spread some icing on top. Cover with second layer and spread remaining icing over top and sides of cake. Sprinkle top with chopped pecans or press halved pecans around the top edge.

Yield: 1 Cake

Servings: 12

Rum Cake

CAKE:

1 butter cake mix (yellow)
1 large package vanilla pudding
¼ cup oil
½ cup water
½ cup rum (white)
4 eggs
½ cup pecans, chopped

GLAZE:

1 cup sugar
1 stick margarine
¼ cup rum
¼ cup water

Grease bundt pan and sprinkle nuts on bottom. Blend cake mix, rum and all other cake ingredients. Pour cake batter over nuts. Bake at 350 degrees for 40-45 minutes. While hot, poke holes in cake with skewer. Boil glaze ingredients and pour over cake. Turn cake out onto serving plate.

Dining Car Special
BOTORKOEK "DUTCH COFFEE CAKE"

3 cups flour
2 cups sugar
2 eggs
1 cup butter
2 teaspoons almond extract
2 teaspoons baking powder
1 cup almonds, slivered

Mix all the ingredients together, except the almonds, until the mixture forms a smooth ball. Divide it into 2 equal parts. Spread each in an ungreased 8-inch cake pan. Spread the dough evenly with your fingers. Make an edge with a fork. Press ½ cup of almonds on top of each cake. Bake at 375 degrees for 30 minutes.

Yield: 2 cakes

Company Coffee Cake

4 cups flour
2 cups brown sugar
$^1/_2$ cup sugar
$^3/_4$ teaspoon salt
2 teaspoons nutmeg
$^3/_4$ cup walnuts, chopped
$1^1/_4$ cups vegetable oil
2 teaspoons cinnamon
2 teaspoons baking soda
1 tablespoon plus 1 teaspoon
   baking powder
3 eggs
2 cups buttermilk

Combine flour, brown sugar, sugar, salt, nutmeg, walnuts and oil in large bowl. Mix until crumbly. Remove 1 $^1/_2$ cups of mixture, stir in cinnamon and set aside for topping. Add baking soda, baking powder, eggs and buttermilk. Blend gently and don't over-mix. Pour into 2 (9x13-inch) baking pans. Sprinkle with topping mixture. Bake at 350 degrees for 30 minutes.

Yield: 2 (9x13-inch) cakes

Note: This recipe works great both as a dessert or a brunch cake.

Best Ever Chocolate Cake

CAKE:

2 cups sugar
$^1/_2$ cup cocoa
1 cup oil
2 eggs
3 cups flour
$^1/_2$ teaspoon salt
1 cup buttermilk
1 teaspoon vanilla
1 cup boiling water
1 teaspoon baking soda

FLUFFY COCOA FROSTING:

$^1/_2$ cup cocoa
3 cups powdered sugar
$^1/_3$ cup butter
1 teaspoon vanilla
$^1/_3$ cup evaporated milk (2% milk
   works)

To make cake: Combine sugar, cocoa, oil, eggs, flour, salt, buttermilk and vanilla and mix well. Add boiling water with baking soda mixed in. Bake at 350 degrees in a 9x13-inch pan for 30-40 minutes or 2 round pans 30 minutes. For cupcakes, bake 15 minutes or mini cupcakes bake 10 minutes. This cake is best if made a day before.

To make frosting: Mix cocoa and sugar. Cream part of cocoa and sugar with butter. Blend in vanilla and $^1/_2$ milk. Add remaining cocoa and sugar. Add remaining milk.

Fudge Cake with Ice Cream & Caramel Sauce

SAUCE:

1   cup sugar
6   tablespoons water
2   teaspoons cream of tartar
$^1/_2$ cup plus 2 tablespoons
     whipping cream
$^1/_4$ cup ($^1/_2$ stick) unsalted butter

CAKE:

$^3/_4$ cup unsweetened cocoa
     powder
1   cup plus 2 tablespoons boiling
     water
$^3/_4$ cup ($1^1/_2$ sticks) unsalted
     butter, room temperature
$2^1/_4$ cups sugar
3   large eggs
$1^1/_2$ teaspoons vanilla extract
$2^1/_4$ cups all-purpose flour
$1^1/_2$ teaspoons baking soda
$^3/_4$ teaspoon salt
$1^1/_2$ cups sour cream

vanilla ice cream

To make sauce: Cook sugar, water and cream of tartar in heavy medium saucepan over medium-low heat, stirring until sugar dissolves. Increase heat to medium-high and cook without stirring until syrup turns deep golden brown, swirling pan occasionally. Remove from heat. Gradually add cream (mixture will bubble vigorously) and stir until smooth. Add butter and whisk until melted. Can be made 1 day ahead. Cover and refrigerate. Before serving, rewarm over low heat until heated through.

To make cake: Preheat oven to 350 degrees. Grease a 9x13-inch baking pan. Place cocoa in metal bowl. Gradually add boiling water, stirring constantly. Cool. Using an electric mixer, cream butter with sugar in large bowl. Add eggs one at a time, beating well after each addition. Beat in vanilla. Mix flour, baking soda and salt in bowl. Stir into butter mixture alternately with sour cream. Stir in cocoa mixture. Pour batter into prepared pan. Bake until toothpick inserted into center of cake comes out clean, about 50 minutes. Cool cake slightly on rack.

Cut warm cake into squares. Divide among plates. Top with scoop of ice cream. Pour caramel sauce over.

Servings: 12

Pumpkin Butterscotch Cake

1   package yellow cake mix
¼   cup vegetable oil
1   package instant butterscotch
     pudding mix
1   cup canned pumpkin
4   eggs
2   teaspoons pumpkin pie spice
¼   cup water
whipped cream

In a large mixing bowl, combine first 7 ingredients. Beat on slow speed for 30 seconds, then on medium speed for 4 minutes. Pour into greased and floured 12-inch bundt pan. Bake at 350 degrees for about 50 minutes. Cool for 15 minutes and then remove from pan and cool completely. Serve with whipped cream.

Yield: 1 (12-inch) bundt cake

Pumpkin Pie Cake

CAKE:

1   box yellow cake mix
½   cup butter or margarine,
     melted
3   eggs
1   (15 ounce) can of pumpkin
⅔   cup sugar
⅔   cup milk
2   teaspoons pumpkin pie spice
1   teaspoon cinnamon

TOPPING:

¼   cup sugar
1   teaspoon cinnamon
¼   cup butter or margarine,
     melted

Remove 1 cup dry cake mix and set aside for topping. Combine remaining cake mix, butter or margarine and 1 egg. Pat into a greased and floured 9x13-inch baking pan for bottom layer. Combine pumpkin, 2 eggs, sugar, milk and spice. Pour over first mixture.

To make topping: Combine reserved cake mix, sugar, cinnamon and butter or margarine. Sprinkle topping crumbs over cake. Bake at 350 degrees for 45 minutes or until tests done.

Suggestion: Great alternative for holiday get-togethers.

Vanilla-Bean Custard Ice Cream

1   cup milk
²/₃   cup sugar
2   vanilla beans, cut in half lengthwise
9   large egg yolks, at room temperature
2   cups heavy cream

Combine milk, sugar and vanilla beans in the top of a double boiler and heat over barely simmering water. Lightly beat the yolks. When milk mixture is almost to the point of boiling, pour a little onto the yolks to warm them. Stir and add a bit more hot milk.

Pour warmed yolks into milk in a slow, steady stream, stirring all the while. Continue to cook, stirring constantly, over hot, not boiling, water until mixture coats the spoon.

Press a sheet of wax paper or cling wrap directly onto the surface of the custard and allow to cool to room temperature.

Add cream to the custard and refrigerate for several hours.

Just before freezing, remove vanilla beans and scrape their seeds into the mixture. Stir and pour into an ice cream maker and freeze according to manufacturer's directions.

Orange Sorbet

1   cup sugar
³/₄   cup water
1   teaspoon grated orange zest
2   cups of fresh orange juice

Mix sugar, water and orange zest in heavy medium saucepan. Bring mixture to boil, stirring to dissolve sugar. Remove from heat. Stir in orange juice and chill for 1 hour. Process mixture in ice cream maker according to manufacturer's instructions. Cover and freeze at least 3 hours or up to 3 days.

Serve with a sprig of mint.

Note: Frozen ice cream/sorbet maker is needed for this recipe.

The Pan Handler - Chilled Strawberry Rhubarb Soup w/Zabaglione Ice Cream

STRAWBERRY RHUBARB SOUP:

1 pound rhubarb, diced
2 cups sugar
2 pounds strawberries, puréed
2 tablespoons kirsch (cherry brandy)

ZABAGLIONE ICE CREAM:

8 egg yolks
5 tablespoons sugar
8 tablespoons Marsala or sweet white wine
3 cups heavy cream
1 tablespoon vanilla extract

STRAWBERRY ZABAGLIONE:

$^1/_2$ cup quartered, hulled strawberries
$^1/_4$ cup plus 3 tablespoons sugar
4 egg yolks
2 teaspoons freshly squeezed lemon juice
1 teaspoon grated lemon zest
1 tablespoon kirsch (cherry brandy)
1 cup heavy cream

Located on Historic 25th Street in Ogden, The Pan Handler offers "everything for the cook" as well as gourmet cooking classes.

To make the soup: Simmer rhubarb, sugar and kirsch for 4 minutes. Add strawberries and simmer 2 minutes. Chill for 3 hours or overnight.

To make the zabaglione ice cream: Separate eggs in a double boiler. Add sugar and Marsala wine. Stir well. Beat the mixture over double boiler for 10 minutes. Be patient and don't let the water boil dry. When the zabaglione is cooked, pour into a bowl and chill until cooled completely. Using a mixer, add heavy cream and vanilla to chilled zabaglione. Blend 2 minutes. Put in ice cream maker and chill according to manufacturer's recommendations.

To make the strawberry zabaglione: Prepare double boiler. Combine the strawberries and the 3 tablespoons sugar in a double boiler and cook over simmering water, stirring occasionally until fruit is tender, about 5 minutes. Remove from heat and let cool. Purée the fruit in a blender or food processor until smooth, about 1 minute.

In a bowl beat the egg yolks and balance of sugar until thick and pale in color. Scrape down the sides of the bowl with a rubber spatula. Whisk in the lemon juice, lemon zest, kirsch and strawberry puree. Transfer the mixture to the double boiler and whisk constantly over barely simmering water for about 5-7 minutes, or until it thickens to a smooth, glossy custard. Remove from heat, cover and refrigerate for at least 1 hour.

In a deep bowl, beat the cream until it forms soft peaks. Using a rubber spatula, fold the chilled custard into the whipped cream. Serve immediately, or cover and refrigerate for up to 3 hours.

To Serve: Pour into individual soup bowls and top with ice cream and strawberry zabaglione.

Wildflour's ~ Famous Pumpkin Cookies with Caramel Frosting

COOKIES:

2   cups shortening
2   cups white sugar
1   (29 ounce) can puréed pumpkin (not pumpkin pie filling)
2   eggs
2   teaspoons vanilla
4   cups all-purpose flour
2   teaspoons baking soda
2   teaspoons baking powder
1   teaspoon salt
2   teaspoons cinnamon

CARAMEL FROSTING:

12 tablespoons butter
1   cup milk
2   cups brown sugar
6+ cups powdered sugar
1   tablespoon vanilla

To make cookies: Cream together shortening and sugar; don't whip. Mix in pumpkin, eggs and vanilla. In a separate bowl, combine flour, soda, baking powder, salt and cinnamon. Add to pumpkin mixture. Bake at 350 degrees for 12-16 minutes. Use an ice cream scoop for a perfect size cookie measure.

To make frosting: Combine butter, milk and brown sugar in a large saucepan. Boil for 2 minutes. Take off heat, let cool. Be sure not to add the powdered sugar until it is really cool. When cool, add powdered sugar and vanilla. Add more powdered sugar if too thin. Frost cookies and serve.

Yield: 42 medium sized cookies

The Wildflour Bakery truly is a part of Ogden's history. Although Past Junior League President and Wildflour Founder, Sally Neill, has moved on to other community opportunities, residents still crave her famous "pumpkin cookies" and the many other delicious cakes, breads and unique desserts that the Wildflour offered. One of her secret recipes is finally out!

Pumpkin Drop Cookies

1/2 cup margarine or butter
1 cup brown sugar
1 egg
1 cup canned pumpkin
1 teaspoon vanilla
2 cups flour
1 teaspoon baking powder
1 teaspoon cinnamon
1/2 teaspoon baking soda
1/2 teaspoon ground nutmeg
1 cup mini-chocolate chips
1/2 cup nuts, chopped (optional)

Using mixer, beat butter and brown sugar until blended. Add egg, pumpkin and vanilla. Beat well. In separate bowl, stir together flour, baking powder, cinnamon, soda and nutmeg. Combine the 2 mixtures, blending well. Stir in chocolate chips and nuts. Spray or grease light colored cookie sheets. Drop dough by teaspoon 2-inches apart. Bake at 375 degrees for 8-10 minutes. Cool on wire rack.

Yield: 3 1/2 dozen cookies

Peanut Butter, Oatmeal, Chocolate Chip Cookies

1 cup soft shortening
1 cup brown sugar
3/4 cup sugar
1 cup peanut butter
2 eggs
2 cups flour
2 teaspoons soda
1/2 teaspoon salt
1 cup oatmeal
1 1/2 cups chocolate chips and/or M&M's® Mini Baking Bits

Cream together sugars, shortening and peanut butter. Add eggs. Mix well. Add flour, soda, salt, oatmeal and chocolate chips. Place large tablespoons of dough on ungreased cookie sheet. Bake at 350 for 10 minutes.

Mother's Chocolate Oatmeal Cookies

$^1/_2$ cup butter, softened

1   cup brown sugar

zest of 1 orange

1   egg unbeaten

$^1/_4$ teaspoon salt

1   teaspoon vanilla

$^1/_2$ cup flour

$1^1/_2$ cups quick oats

1   package semi-sweet chocolate
      chips

Cream together butter and sugar. Add orange zest. Add egg, salt and vanilla; beat well. Stir in flour and oats. Add the chocolate pieces and work into batter. Form into small mounds on a cookie sheet. Bake at 350 degrees for 15 minutes.

Yields: 3 dozen cookies

Banana Oatmeal Cookies

$^3/_4$ cup oil

1   cup sugar

1   egg, beaten

3-4 bananas, mashed

$1^3/_4$ cups quick oats

$1^1/_2$ cups flour

$^1/_2$ teaspoon baking soda

$^3/_4$ teaspoon cinnamon

$^1/_4$ teaspoon nutmeg

pinch of salt

Mix all ingredients in mixer until well mixed. Drop by spoonfuls onto lightly greased cookie sheet. Bake at 350 degrees for 10 minutes. (They don't look very pretty but they are yummy.)

Chocolate Butter Cream Layered Cookies

1½ cups graham cracker crumbs

1 cup walnuts, finely chopped

1 cup plus 1½ tablespoons unsalted butter

¼ cup sugar

½ cup unsweetened baking cocoa

1 egg, beaten

1 teaspoon vanilla extract

2 tablespoons powdered custard or pudding mix

3 tablespoons milk

2 cups confectioners' sugar

4 ounces semisweet baking chocolate

Combine cracker crumbs and walnuts in a food processor or blender. Process until the texture of fine meal. Combine ½ cup butter, sugar, cocoa, egg and vanilla in a saucepan over medium heat; mix well. Cook for 5 minutes or until the consistency of custard, stirring constantly. Combine the crumb mixture and custard mixture in a bowl; mix well. Press into an ungreased 7½x12-inch pan. Place in freezer while making the next layer.

Cream ½ cup butter and custard or pudding mix in a mixing bowl until light and fluffy. Add milk and confectioners' sugar; beat until creamy. Remove first layer from freezer and spread the mixture over the first layer. Return to freezer.

Melt remaining 1½ tablespoons butter and baking chocolate in a small saucepan over low heat. Spread melted chocolate over chilled butter cream layer. Work quickly as chocolate will harden when it touches the cold butter cream. Slice cookies into 1½-inch squares. Store, covered, in the refrigerator for up to 3 weeks or in the freezer for up to 3 months.

Orange Carrot Cookies

COOKIES:

1	cup sugar
$3/4$	cup shortening
1	egg, beaten
1	cup carrots, cooked and mashed
2	cups flour
1	teaspoon baking powder
$1/2$	teaspoon salt
1	teaspoon vanilla

ICING:

1	cup powdered sugar
1	orange zest grated
1	tablespoon orange juice

To make cookies: Cream sugar, shortening and egg. Add mashed carrots, flour, baking powder, salt and vanilla. Mix well. Drop by spoonfuls onto lightly greased cookie sheet. Bake at 375 degrees for 12 minutes.

To make icing: Mix all icing ingredients together until smooth. Drizzle over cooled cookies.

Orange Snowballs

1	cup butter, softened
$3/4$	cup sifted powdered sugar
1	tablespoon orange juice
$2 3/4$	cups all-purpose flour
1	tablespoon plus 2 teaspoons orange zest
$3/4$	cup sugar

In a large mixing bowl, beat butter for 30 seconds. Add powdered sugar; beat. Add orange juice. Beat in as much flour as you can mix with. Use a wooden spoon to stir in 1 tablespoon orange zest and remaining flour.

Shape dough into $1 1/4$-inch balls. Place 2-inches apart on ungreased cookie sheet. Bake at 325 degrees for 15 minutes. Cool for 5 minutes.

In a food processor combine $3/4$ cup sugar and 2 teaspoons orange zest. Roll the baked cookies in sugar mixture.

Yield: 48 balls

Never Fail Roll-Out Sugar Cookies

COOKIES:

1¼ cups sugar

1   cup shortening or ½ cup shortening and ½ cup butter

2   eggs

½   cup milk minus 3 tablespoons

1   teaspoon vanilla

4   cups flour

½   teaspoon salt

1   teaspoon baking powder

½   teaspoon soda

FROSTING:

¼   cup butter, softened

1   (8 ounce) package cream cheese, softened

1   tablespoon vanilla

3½ cups powdered sugar

To make cookies: Cream sugar and shortening/butter mixture together. Add eggs and cream until smooth; set aside. Add vanilla to the milk; set aside. In a separate bowl, mix together flour, salt, baking powder and soda.

Alternately, add the milk and flour mixture to the sugar and shortening mixture. Chill the cookie dough for at least 3 hours.

Roll and cut into your favorite design. Bake at 350 degrees for 10-12 minutes.

To make Frosting: Combine butter and cream cheese. Add vanilla. Slowly stir in powdered sugar. Stir until smooth and creamy.

Grandma's Soft Sugar Cookies

¼   cup butter

1½ cups white sugar

2   eggs

1   teaspoon vanilla

3   cups sifted flour

1   teaspoon salt

½   teaspoon baking powder

½   teaspoon baking soda

1   cup sour cream

cinnamon sugar

Cream butter. Add sugar gradually. Add eggs one at a time. Add vanilla. Mix flour, salt, baking powder and baking soda together. Add to the creamed mixture alternately with sour cream beginning and ending with dry ingredients. Drop by spoonfuls onto greased cookie sheet. With a spatula dipped in flour, flatten into circles and sprinkle with cinnamon sugar. Bake at 350 degrees for 8-10 minutes.

Chocolate Ginger Molasses Crinkles

$^2/_3$ cup shortening
1   cup sugar
1   egg
$^1/_4$ cup molasses
$2^1/_4$ cups flour
1   tablespoon ground ginger
$1^1/_2$ teaspoons baking soda
$^1/_4$ teaspoon salt
2   (1 ounce) squares of chocolate
     unsweetened, melted and
     cooled
sugar

Cream shortening and sugar, beating well. Add egg and beat well. Stir in molasses. In a separate bowl, combine flour, ginger, soda and salt, stir well. Add to creamed mixture. Stir in melted chocolate. Shape dough into 1-inch balls; roll balls in sugar. Bake at 350 degrees for 10-12 minutes.

Yields: 4 dozen

Soft Ginger Snaps

1   egg, beaten
1   cup sugar
$^1/_4$ cup molasses
$^3/_4$ cup oil
2   teaspoons baking soda
$^1/_4$ teaspoon salt
1   teaspoon ground cloves
1   teaspoon ground cinnamon
$1^1/_2$ teaspoon ground ginger
2   cups unsifted flour
sugar

Beat egg well. Add sugar, molasses and oil; beat well. Add soda, salt and spices; beat well. Add flour and mix until well blended. Roll dough into balls the size of a quarter and dip top in granulated sugar. Place sugar side up on greased cookie sheet. Bake at 350 degrees for 10-12 minutes.

Chewy Chocolate-Gingerbread Cookies

7 ounces semisweet chocolate

1$\frac{1}{2}$ cups plus 1 tablespoon all-purpose flour

1$\frac{1}{4}$ teaspoons ground ginger

1 teaspoon ground cinnamon

$\frac{1}{4}$ teaspoon ground cloves

$\frac{1}{4}$ teaspoon ground nutmeg

1 tablespoon cocoa powder

8 tablespoons (1 stick) unsalted butter

1 tablespoon ginger, freshly grated

$\frac{1}{2}$ cup dark-brown sugar, packed

$\frac{1}{4}$ cup unsulfured molasses

1 teaspoon baking soda

1$\frac{1}{2}$ teaspoons boiling water

$\frac{1}{4}$ cup granulated sugar

Line 2 baking sheets with parchment. Chop chocolate into $\frac{1}{4}$-inch chunks; set aside. In medium bowl, sift together flour, ginger, cinnamon, cloves, nutmeg and cocoa.

In a bowl with an electric mixer, beat butter and grated ginger until whitened, about 4 minutes. Add brown sugar; beat until combined. Add molasses; beat until combined.

In a small bowl, dissolve baking soda in boiling water. Beat half of flour mixture into butter mixture. Beat in baking soda mixture, then remaining half of flour mixture. Mix in chocolate; turn out onto a piece of plastic wrap. Pat dough out to about 1-inch thick; seal with wrap; refrigerate until firm, 2 hours or more.

Heat oven to 325 degrees. Roll dough into 1$\frac{1}{2}$-inch balls, place 2-inches apart on baking sheets. Refrigerate 20 minutes. Roll in granulated sugar. Bake until the surfaces crack slightly, 13-15 minutes; let cool 5 minutes; transfer to a wire rack to cool completely.

Big Soft Ginger Cookies

2¼ cups flour
2 teaspoons ground ginger
1 teaspoon baking soda
¾ teaspoon ground cinnamon
½ teaspoon ground cloves
¼ teaspoon salt (optional)
¾ cup margarine, butter or shortening
1 cup sugar
1 egg
¼ cup molasses
2 tablespoons sugar

Combine flour, ginger, soda, cinnamon, cloves and salt; set aside. In a large mixing bowl, beat margarine, butter or shortening with an electric mixer on low speed for 30 seconds to soften. Gradually add sugar; beat until fluffy. Add egg and molasses; beat well. Stir dry ingredients into wet mixture.

Shape into 1½-inch balls (1 heaping tablespoon dough each). Roll in the 2 tablespoons sugar and place on an ungreased cookie sheet about 2½-inches apart. Bake at 350 degrees for 10 minutes or until light brown and still puffed. (Do not overcook). Let stand 2 minutes before transferring to a wire rack. Cool.

Yields: 24 (3-inch) cookies

Cream Filled Swedish Wafers

COOKIES:
1 cup butter
⅓ cup heavy cream
2 cups flour

FROSTING:
½ cup butter, softened
1 cup powdered sugar
1 teaspoon vanilla
dash almond extract

Mix butter, cream and flour together as for piecrust. Chill for at least ½ hour.

Roll ⅛-inch thick. Cut into 1½-inch rounds and dip both sides in granulated sugar. Place on cookie sheet. Prick with fork. Bake at 375 degrees for about 7-9 minutes. Cool and put 2 wafers together with frosting to make cream filled sandwich cookie.

To make frosting: Combine all ingredients until well blended.

Peanut Butter Fingers

COOKIES:

$^1/_2$ cup butter, softened

$^1/_2$ cup margarine, softened

1 cup sugar

1 cup brown sugar

1 cup peanut butter

2 eggs

1 teaspoon baking soda

$^1/_2$ teaspoon salt

2 cups flour

2 cups oats

$^1/_2$ cup peanut butter

FROSTING:

$^1/_2$ cup butter (melted)

4 tablespoons cocoa

6 tablespoons milk

$3^1/_2$ cups powdered sugar

1 teaspoon vanilla

To make cookies: Blend butter, margarine, sugars and peanut butter. Add eggs, soda, salt, flour and oats. Mix well. Spread out on a large cookie sheet. Bake at 350 degrees for 15 minutes. Cool.

To make frosting: Mix butter, cocoa, milk, sugar and vanilla together. Beat until light and fluffy.

Spread with peanut butter and then frosting on top.

Dining Car Special
MELT-AWAYS

COOKIES:

1 cup butter

$^3/_4$ cup sifted cornstarch

$^1/_3$ cup powdered sugar

1 cup flour

FROSTING:

3 ounces cream cheese

1 teaspoon vanilla

1 cup powdered sugar

2 drops of milk

2 drops of food coloring

Beat butter until very soft. Add cornstarch, sugar and flour. Mix very well. Drop $^1/_2$-1-inch balls onto ungreased cookie sheet. Bake at 350 degrees for 10-12 minutes or until set and very lightly browned. Cool on a wire rack in a single layer, never stacked or overlapped.

Combine all ingredients for frosting and beat until smooth. Drop a dab on top of each cookie.

Chocolate Chip Squares

1   cup shortening
¹/₂ cup white sugar
¹/₂ cup brown sugar
2   egg yolks
¹/₄ teaspoon salt
¹/₂ teaspoon baking powder
2   cups flour
24 ounces chocolate chips
1   cup nuts, chopped

MERINGUE:

2   egg whites
1   cup brown sugar
1   pinch baking powder

Cream shortening and sugars, then add 2 egg yolks; reserve egg whites. Sift salt, baking powder and flour. Combine with creamed mixture. Spread in a 9x13-inch pan and sprinkle with chocolate chips and chopped nuts.

To make meringue: Beat reserved egg whites stiff then beat in brown sugar and baking powder. Spread meringue on chocolate chips and chopped nuts. Bake at 350 degrees for 5 minutes and then decrease oven temperature to 300 degrees for 15-20 minutes. Cool and cut into squares.

Hip Loader Bars

FILLING:

1   (14 ounce) can sweetened
    condensed milk
6   ounces chocolate chips
2   tablespoons butter
1   teaspoon vanilla

CRUST:

¹/₂ cup butter, softened
1   cup brown sugar
1   egg
1¹/₄ cups flour
1¹/₂ cups quick cooking oatmeal
¹/₄ teaspoon salt
¹/₂ teaspoon baking soda
1   teaspoon vanilla

In a saucepan mix milk, chocolate chips, butter and vanilla. Heat to melt butter and chocolate chips. Stir well. Set aside.

Cut softened butter into sugar. Add egg, flour, oatmeal, salt, soda and vanilla. Press ²/₃ of mix into a greased 8x8-inch pan. Pour chocolate mix over top and crumble remaining crust over top. Bake at 350 degrees for 25 minutes.

Luscious Lemon Bars

CRUST:

1 cup butter, softened (do not use margarine)

$^1/_2$ cup powdered sugar

dash salt

2 cups flour

FILLING:

4 eggs, beaten

2 cups granulated sugar

$^1/_4$ cup flour

6 tablespoons lemon juice

powdered sugar

To make crust: Combine all crust ingredients in a bowl and mix well. Press flat into ungreased 9x13-inch pan. Bake at 350 degrees for 15 minutes until lightly browned.

To make filling: Combine flour and sugar. Mix in beaten eggs and lemon juice. Pour into slightly cooled crust and bake at 350 degrees for 25 minutes or until set.

Cool and sprinkle lightly with powdered sugar.

Pecan Pie Bars

2 cups all-purpose flour

$^1/_2$ cup sugar

$^1/_8$ teaspoon salt

$^3/_4$ cup butter, cut up

1 cup brown sugar, packed

1 cup light corn syrup

$^1/_2$ cup butter

4 large eggs, lightly beaten

$2^1/_2$ cups pecans, finely chopped

1 teaspoon vanilla extract

Combine flour, sugar and salt in a large bowl; cut in $^3/_4$ cup butter thoroughly with a pastry blender until mixed and resembling fine crumbs. Press mix evenly into a greased 9x13-inch pan, using a piece of plastic wrap to press crumb mixture firmly in pan. Bake at 350 degrees for 17-20 minutes or until lightly browned.

Combine brown sugar, corn syrup and $^1/_2$ cup butter in saucepan and bring to a boil over medium heat, stirring gently. Remove from heat. Stir $^1/_4$ of hot mixture into beaten eggs: add remaining hot mixture. Stir in pecans and vanilla. Pour filling over crust. Bake at 350 degrees for 30-35 minutes or until set. Cool completely in pan on a wire rack. Cut into bars.

Yields: 16 large bars

Baby Food Bars

BARS:

3   eggs

1$^1/_2$ cups vegetable oil

2   cups sugar

1   teaspoon salt

2   cups flour

2   teaspoons baking soda

1   (4$^1/_2$ ounce) jar strained apricots baby food

1   (4$^1/_2$ ounce) jar applesauce baby food

1   (4$^1/_2$ ounce) jar strained carrots baby food

2   teaspoons ground cinnamon

FROSTING:

1   stick butter, softened

1   (8 ounce) package cream cheese, softened

4   cups powdered sugar

1   teaspoon vanilla

Beat eggs and oil. Combine all ingredients and beat. Pour in a 9x13-inch pan and bake at 350 degrees for 30 minutes. Cool.

To make frosting: Combine all ingredients and beat until creamy.

Frost, cut into bars and serve.

Dining Car Special
NUTTY PINEAPPLE

1   medium-size ripe pineapple

$^1/_4$ cup butter or margarine

$^1/_4$ cup coconut, shredded

2   tablespoons almonds, finely chopped

1   tablespoon light brown sugar

Cut off leafy top of pineapple. Cut pineapple lengthwise into 6 wedges; cut off the core of each wedge. Slash the flesh vertically down to, but not through, the skin at $^1/_2$-inch intervals.

In small saucepan heat butter until melted. Brush half over wedges. To butter remaining in saucepan, add coconut, almonds and brown sugar; stir until well mixed. Spoon some mixture into slashes.

Place pineapple on grill over medium coals, cut-side down. Grill 5 minutes, turn and grill 5 more minutes until lightly browned and heated thoroughly.

Servings: 6

Coconut Cranberry Chews

$1^{1}/_{2}$ cups butter or margarine at
    room temperature
2   cups sugar
1   tablespoon orange zest
2   teaspoons vanilla
$3^{1}/_{4}$ cups all-purpose flour
1   teaspoon baking powder
$^{1}/_{4}$ teaspoon salt
$1^{1}/_{2}$ cups dried cranberries
$1^{1}/_{2}$ cups sweetened coconut

In large mixing bowl beat butter, sugar, orange zest and vanilla until smooth and fluffy; set aside.

In a medium bowl mix flour, baking powder and salt. Add to butter mixture, stir on low to mix, then beat on low until dough comes together; mixture will look dry. Mix in cranberries and coconut.

Shape dough into one-inch balls, press with fork. Bake at 350 degrees for about 12 minutes, just until edges brown lightly.

Raspberry Torte

1   cup butter
1   cup sugar
1   egg yolk
1   whole egg
$^{1}/_{2}$ teaspoon baking soda
2   cups flour
1   cup nuts, chopped
raspberry jam

Cream butter until soft. Add sugar; cream until fluffy. Add eggs; blend well. Gradually add soda and flour; mix well. Fold in nuts. Spread $^{1}/_{2}$ the batter into an 8-inch square pan, top evenly with jam, cover with remaining dough. Bake at 350 degrees for 45 minutes or until lightly brown.

Raspberry Dessert

CRUST:

2¹/₄ cups flour

2 tablespoons sugar

³/₄ cup butter, softened

FILLING:

1 (8 ounce) package of cream cheese, softened

1 cup powdered sugar

1 teaspoon vanilla

¹/₄ teaspoon salt

1 (8 ounce) tub whipped topping

TOPPING:

2 cups boiling water

1 (16 ounce) package raspberry gelatin

2 (10 ounce) packages sweetened frozen raspberries

To make crust: Mix together flour and sugar. Blend in butter until smooth. Press into a 9x13-inch baking pan. Bake at 300 degrees for 20 minutes, or until set (will not be brown). Cool.

To make filling: Beat cream cheese, powdered sugar, vanilla and salt till smooth. Gently fold in whipped topping. Spread evenly over crust.

To make topping: Dissolve gelatin in boiling water. Stir in raspberries. Chill in refrigerator for 15 minutes, or until gelatin begins to thicken. Spoon over filling. Refrigerate until set. To serve, cut into squares and garnish with whipped topping and mint leaves, if desired.

Servings: 12-16

Spiced Baked Rhubarb

4 cups rhubarb, cut

1 cup sugar (or more)

4 whole cloves

Preheat oven to 400 degrees. Place rhubarb in an oven safe dish (with cover). Cover rhubarb with sugar and cloves. Bake covered for 25 minutes or until tender.

Pear Raspberry Cobbler

1¹/₂ cups sifted all-purpose flour

¹/₄ teaspoon salt, scant

5   tablespoons solid vegetable shortening, frozen

¹/₄ cup unsalted butter, frozen

4-5 tablespoons ice water

6   cups firm pears, peeled, cored and sliced

1¹/₄ cups fresh raspberries

³/₄ cup sugar

¹/₄ cup unsalted butter, cut into bits

Preheat oven to 425 degrees. Grease a deep 7x9-inch ovenproof dish. Set aside.

Combine flour, salt, frozen shortening and butter in a food processor fitted with a metal blade. Process until the mixture is rough textured. Add water slowly and process until dough begins to cling together. Gather into a ball and place between 2 sheets of wax paper, flattening the ball slightly. Refrigerate for 30 minutes.

Roll out dough into a rough rectangle and line the bottom and sides of the prepared dish, letting excess crust drape over the edge. Heap pears into dish, mounding slightly in the middle. Sprinkle the berries evenly over the dish and then pour sugar evenly over all. Dot with butter. Bring dough up and let it flop over fruit, using any that falls off to patch the middle.

Bake for 45 minutes, or until golden brown. Serve with cream or ice cream.

Serves: 6-8

Mother's Apple Crisp

5-6 apples
1 cup flour
1 cup sugar
1 teaspoon baking powder
$^1/_4$ teaspoon salt
1 unbeaten egg
1 stick butter, melted
cinnamon

Place sliced pared apples in an 8x8-inch baking dish.

Mix together flour, sugar, baking powder, salt and egg with fork until crumbly and sprinkle over the apples; top with melted butter. Sprinkle with cinnamon. Bake at 350 degrees for 30 minutes.

Serve warm with ice cream.

Tartlet Shells

$^1/_2$ cup butter, softened
1 small package cream cheese, softened
2 tablespoons powdered sugar
1 tablespoon brandy
$1^1/_4$ cups flour
lemon curd or chocolate pudding

Combine butter, cream cheese and powdered sugar. Beat until light and fluffy. Blend in brandy. Gradually add flour and blend until smooth. Form into tartlet pans and bake at 350 degrees for 8 minutes or lightly brown. Fill with lemon curd or chocolate pudding.

Chocolate Cream Raspberry Tart

TART:

1½ cups graham cracker crumbs

4 tablespoons reduced-calorie stick margarine

1½ tablespoons sugar

1½ teaspoons vanilla extract

½ teaspoon ground cinnamon

FILLING:

1½ teaspoons unflavored gelatin

1 cup 1% low-fat milk

½ cup sugar

2½ tablespoons cornstarch

2 tablespoons unsweetened cocoa

⅛ teaspoon salt

¼ cup semisweet chocolate morsels

¾ teaspoon vanilla extract

¼ teaspoon almond extract

1½ cups reduced-calorie frozen whipped topping, thawed

3 cups fresh raspberries

¼ cup red currant jelly, melted

To make tart: Combine cracker crumbs, margarine, sugar, vanilla extract and cinnamon; stir well. Press mixture into bottom and up the sides of a 9-inch round removable bottom tart pan. Bake at 350 degrees for 11 minutes; cool on a wire rack.

To make filling: Combine gelatin and ¼ cup milk in a bowl; set aside.

Combine sugar, cornstarch, unsweetened cocoa and salt. Gradually add remaining ¾ cup milk, stirring with a wire whisk. Bring to a boil over medium-low heat and cook 1 minute, stirring constantly. Remove from heat; add chocolate morsels, stirring until chocolate melts. Stir in extracts.

Add chocolate mixture to gelatin mixture (in bowl), stirring until gelatin dissolves. Place bowl over a large ice filled bowl, stir 10 minutes or until cool; remove from ice-filled bowl. Add whipped topping, stirring gently until well blended. Spoon evenly into tart shell. Arrange raspberries on top of tart. Gently brush raspberries with melted jelly. Chill 2 hours before serving.

Servings: 9

White Chocolate Cheesecake

CRUST:

2   cups chocolate wafer crumbs

2   tablespoons sugar

$^1/_3$ cup butter, melted

CHEESECAKE:

4   (8 ounce) packages cream cheese, softened

1   cup sugar

4   large eggs

$^1/_2$ cup Irish Crème liqueur or half-and-half

1   tablespoon vanilla extract

$^1/_2$ pound white chocolate, chopped

To make crust: Combine chocolate wafer crumbs, sugar and butter in a medium bowl; stir well. Press mixture firmly on bottom and 2-inches up side of a 10-inch spring form pan. Bake at 325 degrees for 6-8 minutes. Set aside to cool.

To make cheesecake: Beat cream cheese until smooth. Add sugar, beating well. Add eggs, one at a time, beating just until blended after each addition. Stir in liqueur and vanilla. Add white chocolate; stir well. Pour mixture into prepared crust. Bake at 325 degrees for 50-60 minutes until set. Turn oven off. Partially open oven door. Leave cheesecake in oven 1 hour. Remove cake from oven; let cool to room temperature in pan on a wire rack. Cover and chill thoroughly. To serve, remove sides of spring form pan.

Garnish with marbled chocolate curls.

To make marbled chocolate curls: Melt 12 ounces semi-sweet chocolate in top of double boiler over hot water. Pour onto a smooth surface like marble or an aluminum foil-lined baking sheet. Melt 12 ounces of white chocolate and pour over semi-sweet layer. Using a small spatula, swirl chocolates to create a marble effect covering a 12x9-inch area. Let chocolate stand at room temperature until it feels slightly tacky but not firm. Pull a cheese plane across chocolate to form curls.

Yield: 1 (10-inch) cheesecake

Rich Lemon Sauce

$^1/_3$ cup butter
1 cup sugar
3 egg yolks, slightly beaten
$^1/_3$ cup boiling water
3 tablespoons fresh lemon juice
1 teaspoon lemon zest

Cream butter and sugar. Add egg yolks and water. Cook on top of double boiler over boiling water, or in a heavy saucepan, stirring constantly, until thick. Add lemon juice and zest. Serve warm or cold over cake such as angel food or pound cake.

Note: For vanilla sauce, substitute 1 teaspoon vanilla for lemon juice and zest.

Sabayon Topping

4 egg yolks
3 tablespoons sugar
3 tablespoons flour
1 cup half-and-half
$^1/_4$ cup amaretto (or 1 teaspoon almond flavoring)
dash of salt

In double boiler beat egg yolks, add sugar and blend; add flour and beat, gradually add half-and-half, beat. Cook over low heat stirring constantly. Add amaretto and salt. Heat until thick. Remove from heat.

Serve over fresh fruit, ice cream or cheese cake.

Dining Car Special
SOUR CREAM FUDGE

32 ounces of white chocolate
1 (7 ounce) jar marshmallow cream
1 tablespoon vanilla
2 cups walnuts, chopped
4 cups sugar
$^1/_4$ pound butter
1 pint sour cream

Combine white chocolate, marshmallow cream, vanilla and nuts. Set aside. Combine sugar, butter and sour cream in saucepan. Heat until mixture boils, stirring constantly. Cook 5 minutes while boiling. Fold into chocolate mixture until smooth. Pour into buttered 9x13-inch dish. Cool in refrigerator. Cut into pieces.

Hard Candy

3³/₄ cups sugar
1¹/₄ cups white corn syrup
1 cup water
1¹/₂ teaspoons flavoring oils
food coloring
powdered sugar

Cook sugar, corn syrup and water to 300 degrees. Add flavoring and coloring. Stir well and pour into 1-2 cookie sheets which have been covered with quite a bit of powdered sugar. As soon as cool enough to handle, break into bite-sized pieces.

Flavoring oils can be purchased at a pharmacy. Recommended flavors: cinnamon (red food coloring), spearmint (green food coloring), peppermint (yellow food coloring). Great for Christmas!

Graham Cracker Toffee

2 sticks butter (or one margarine and one butter)
1 cup light brown sugar, firmly packed
pinch salt
graham crackers
¹/₂ cup pecans, chopped

Combine butter, brown sugar and salt in a saucepan and bring to a boil for 4 minutes.

Place 24 graham crackers in a foil-lined cookie sheet. Pour hot syrup over crackers, sprinkle chopped pecans on top. Bake at 350 degrees for 10 minutes. Cool and break into pieces.

Divinity

4 cups white sugar
1¼ cups water
1 cup white corn syrup
3 extra large egg whites
1 cup walnuts (optional)

Boil sugar, water and syrup until hard crack stage (pour 1 teaspoon of the boiling syrup into a cup of ice water and when you pick up the hardened syrup it should make a cracking sound on side of cup). Beat the egg whites until very stiff. Pour boiled mixture over the beaten whites and beat with electric mixer until very stiff. Add walnuts and gently stir in. Spoon dollops onto aluminum foil and cool.

Tip: If it becomes too dry you can add 1 teaspoon boiling water.

Caramel Popcorn

3 bags microwave popcorn (cooked to perfection), lightly salted/buttered
1 stick unsalted butter
1 can sweetened condensed milk
½ cup light corn syrup
½ cup creamed honey
16 ounces brown sugar

Cook all ingredients except popcorn together on medium heat until mixed and caramel makes a soft ball in a cup of water. Pour over popcorn, mixing throughout and serve immediately.

Sesame Nut Crunch

1/2 cup unsalted butter
1 cup packed brown sugar
1/4 cup light corn syrup
1 3/4 teaspoons cayenne pepper
1/2 teaspoon salt
2 1/2 cups salted roasted peanuts
2 1/2 cups salted roasted cashews
1/2 cup roasted sunflower nuts
3 tablespoons sesame seeds

Over medium heat, stir butter, sugar, syrup, cayenne and salt until melted and smooth, about 5 minutes. Add nuts and seeds. Increase heat to medium high. Stir until very thick and nuts begin to brown, about 5 minutes. Pour onto buttered piece of foil. Spread. Cool about 15 minutes. Break into pieces and store in an air tight container.

Sweet Chex® Mix

1/2 box Corn Chex®
1/4 box Wheat Chex®
1/4 box Rice Chex®
12 ounces mixed, salted nuts
6 ounces salted, sunflower nuts
1 1/2 cups sugar
1 1/2 cups dark corn syrup
1 1/8 cups butter
2 teaspoons vanilla

Combine cereals and nuts in a large bowl and set aside. Boil sugar, corn syrup and butter for 2 minutes. Remove from heat and add vanilla. Pour over cereal and nuts covering completely. Spread on wax paper to cool.

Spiked Watermelon Salad

1   (8 pound) watermelon, peeled
    cut into 1-inch pieces (about
    16 cups)
1   cup fresh lemon juice
²⁄₃ cup sugar
¹⁄₂ cup vodka
6   tablespoons crème de cassis
¹⁄₄ cup fresh mint, chopped

Place watermelon in large bowl. Whisk fresh lemon juice and sugar in medium bowl until sugar dissolves. Whisk in vodka and crème de cassis. Season mixture to taste with salt. Pour mixture over watermelon. Cover and chill at least one hour and up to 2 hours. Sprinkle with chopped fresh mint and serve.

Suggestion: Use red or yellow watermelon (or both) for this summery dessert and pair it with brownies.

Dining Car Special
BAKED APPLES WITH BRANDY CREAM TOPPING

APPLES:

4   large apples (1¹⁄₂ pounds),
    peeled and sliced thin
1   teaspoon lemon juice
¹⁄₄ - ¹⁄₂ cup sugar (depending on
    taste)
3   tablespoons butter
¹⁄₂ cup heavy cream

TOPPING:

3   ounces cream cheese (room
    temperature)
¹⁄₂ cup heavy cream
¹⁄₄ cup sugar
1   tablespoon brandy

Butter 1 ¹⁄₂ quart glass baking dish. Place apples in dish, sprinkle with lemon juice and sugar. Mix to distribute sugar. Dot with butter. Bake in pre-heated oven 400 degrees for ¹⁄₂ hour. Turn oven to 500 degrees, pour cream over apples and bake 5 minutes or until golden brown. Serve with brandy cream sauce topping.

Topping: Beat cream cheese and cream together. Add sugar and beat until smooth. Blend in brandy.

Servings: 4-6

Dining Car Special
LICORICE CARAMELS

1   cup butter or margarine
1   (14 ounce) can sweetened
     condensed milk
1$^1/_2$ cups light corn syrup
$^1/_4$ teaspoon salt
2   cups sugar
$^3/_4$ teaspoon black food paste
     coloring
$^3/_4$ teaspoon anise oil or anise
     flavoring

Slowly melt butter in heavy large pan. Use fork to swirl butter up sides of pan to prevent sugar crystals. When melted, add rest of ingredients, except food paste and flavoring. Turn heat to medium – medium high, cook and stir constantly with flat bottom wooden spoon. (Do not cook on high, stir the whole time.) Cook to 234 degrees. Remove from heat; add food paste and flavoring, mix in. Pour into 9x13-inch pan that has been buttered. Let set overnight in a cool place. Cut in squares and wrap in waxed paper.

Yield: 50-60 Caramels

TIPS:

To easily remove caramels from the pan: Lay a flat piece of foil on the counter and butter generously. Press the foil into 9x13-inch pan and then pour the hot caramel into the pan. When cool, lift foil out, turn onto cutting board, remove foil and cut into squares. Then wrap in waxed paper.

To make plain caramels: Omit anise and black food coloring paste and substitute with 2 teaspoons of vanilla.

To make delicious caramel apples: Omit anise and black food coloring paste and substitute with 2 teaspoons of vanilla. Dip your apples in caramel and set on a piece of waxed paper on a cookie sheet.

To make delicious caramel fondue: Omit anise and black food coloring paste and substitute with 2 teaspoons of vanilla. Serve warm and dip bananas, apples or whatever you choose.

Notes:

Acknowledgements

JUNIOR LEAGUE OF OGDEN
BOARD OF DIRECTORS 2002- 2003

April Boyer
President

Colleen Letendre
Marketing Vice President

Amanda Freeman
Treasurer

Nicole Boucher
President-Elect

Tara Jorgenson
Membership Vice President

Wendy Toliver
Recording Secretary

Lori Weidner
Community Vice President

Debbie Campbell
Finance Vice President

Zee Conroy
Sustaining Director

*Junior League of Ogden wishes to thank everyone
who assisted with gathering, testing and editing recipes*

WE GRATEFULLY ACKNOWLEDGE THE GENEROUS
CONTRIBUTIONS TO *JLO ART OF COOKING*
FROM THE FOLLOWING LOCAL ARTISTS:

Julie Lewis
cover art, page 1, 130

Liz Pierce
page 6, 129

Blanche P. Wilson
page 41, 74

Scott Wallis
page 13, 25, 45, 145

Marama H. Hansen
page 73

Shanna Kunz
page 42, 52

David W. Jackson
page 89

Cara Koolmees
page 26

Brandon Cook
page 90

Terry C. Johnson
page 3, 104, 146

Steve Songer
page 5

Debra Marin
page 2

JUNIOR LEAGUE OF OGDEN
ACTIVE MEMBERS 2002-2003

Dianne Anderson

Lisa Anderson

Lisa Lynne Arbogast

Catherine Bachtar

Laura Bafford

Suzette Baldazo

Gina Bell

Eden Betz

Rebecca Beyer

Nicole Boucher

April Boyer

Mara Brown

Anita Brzowski

Gillian Burton

Kym Buttschardt

Debbie Campbell

Heather Carlson

Keicha Chapman

Stephanie Christiansen

Laura D'Hulst

Kimberly Young Doman

Paulette Eschler

Cathy Fennell

Rainie Finch

Trish Fine

Linda Flint

Amanda Freeman

Kim Girz

Brenda Goddard

Telitha Greiner

Julie Halsall

Monica Hambleton

Nikki Harris

Casree Holland

Jodi Holmgren

Kyra Hudson

Stacy Johnson

Tara Jorgenson

Kristen Kenley

Melanie Lee

Colleen Letendre

Kelly Lowrey

Denise Lyon

Nancy McLeod

Sue McMickell

Christine Melvick

Karyn Minkevitch

Sondra Motes

Tiffany Nash

Heidi Novak

Yvonne Parkin

Becky Parson

Cathy Parsons

Ranae Poelman

Becky Pulliam

Kim Redd

Tracy Rich-Greiner

Heather Rigby

Kathie Robinson

Rosemarie 'Roe' Schoof

Diane 'Di' Sedgwick

Karen Senn

Bonnie Smith

Amy Sondrup

Diane Neri Stern

Corina Thoits

Melanie Tobias

Sara Toliver

Wendy Toliver

Vanessa Watson

Lori Weidner

Megan Welton

Marian Wharton

Sue Wilkerson

Kellie Woods

Herb Chart

ALLSPICE

Allspice has a delicate flavor resembling a blend of cloves, cinnamon and nutmeg. It is good for (whole) pickles, meats, boiled fish, gravies; (ground) puddings, relishes, fruit preserves and baking.

BASIL

Fresh basil has a sweet clove-like flavor. Dried basil has a flavor that leans more toward anise and lemon. While dried basil is worlds apart from fresh, it can be substituted in cooked dishes and simmered sauces. Never substitute dried for fresh in an uncooked dish. It is good with tomatoes, pasta, pesto, shrimp and fish, most vegetables, beans, soups and salad dressings.

BAY LEAVES

Bay leaves are a sweet, herbaceous floral spice. They are best when dried. Bay leaves are perfect for pickling, stews, for spicing sauces and soup. Also use with a variety of meats and fish.

CAYENNE PEPPER

Cayenne pepper consists of thin, red & yellow very hot peppers and can be used whole, or dried and ground. Great in meats, soups, sauces, chili, seafood, Mexican & Cajun dishes.

CARAWAY

Caraway combines the flavor of both anise and dill. It can be used in kummel and baking breads. It is often added to sauerkraut, noodles and cheese spreads. Also adds zest to French fried potatoes, liver, canned asparagus.

CHIVES

Chives have a slightly sweet, light onion flavor and lift many foods above the mundane. They are best fresh. Chives go well with soft cheeses, vegetables, salad dressings, potatoes, egg dishes such as omelets, soup and fish. They also taste great in herb butters.

CURRY POWDER

Curry powder is a ground blend of as many as 16 to 20 spices. Curry recipes include lamb, chicken, rice, eggs, vegetables and curry puffs.

DILL

Fresh dill has a sweet, full aroma. The seeds are delicious fresh or dried. The leaves are best used fresh, but may be used dry. Dill is great in pickled cucumbers, breads, pasta, coleslaw, scrambled eggs, potato salad and cream soups.

FENNEL

Fennel has a pronounced aniseed flavor, with its seeds having the strongest flavor; dried fennel loses most of its flavor. The seeds, leaves and bulbs are all used in cooking. Mix with thyme and parsley to create an herb butter for fish, or mix with rosemary and garlic for roasted pork. Great in breads, sauces and soups. Seeds are a main seasoning in Italian sausage.

GARLIC

Fresh garlic is strongest when first cut or mashed and used raw. Roasted garlic has a more mellow taste. Use with sauces, dressings, meats, fish, poultry and tomato dishes. Cut a clove in half and rub cut side on inner surface of salad bowl before adding fresh salad for just a hint of flavor.

MARJORAM

Fresh and dried marjoram are both delicious, possessing a distinctive savory flavor. A cousin to the stronger oregano, marjoram is good with any robust-flavored food. Use in butter sauces for fish, with cheese, chopped meats, soups, stews, potatoes, pasta, rice and most vegetables.

MINT

Mint has a clean, sharp flavor and is best used fresh, with peppermint being the most popular choice. Use fresh leaves in both fruit and vegetable salads, creamy fruit soups and when making mint jelly. Rub fresh leaves on poultry before baking.

NUTMEG

Nutmeg tastes like the holidays and most people add it to holiday spirits like mulled wine, eggnog and cider, as its warm, sweet flavor is a pleasant addition. In addition to holiday beverages, baked sweets and puddings, nutmeg is often paired with cheese dishes, fillings, creamy sauces, creamed spinach and mashed potatoes.

OREGANO

Oregano is a very popular herb, especially in Italian cooking. Use in pizzas, meats, beans, sauces, soups and fresh mushrooms. It couples well with tomatoes, eggs and cheeses and can be used fresh, dried or frozen.

PARSLEY

Flat-leaf (Italian) parsley is known for its flavor, whereas curly parsley is most often used for plate garnishing. Add parsley toward the end of the cooking time to soups, sauces, egg dishes, salads, creamed potatoes and marinades. Sprinkle over vegetables, hot cooked rice, pasta and potatoes.

ROSEMARY

Rosemary is an aromatic resinous leaf which aids the digestion of fats in foods such as lamb and pork. It is delicious in breads and biscuits, soups, egg dishes, baked fish, meats, basting sauces and poultry. Dried rosemary retains its flavor well.

SAGE

Sage has a strong, pungent flavor that's best when used lightly in foods. It's a classic in turkey stuffing and in poultry seasoning blends. Mix sage with fennel and use with fish, veal and sausage.

TARRAGON

Tarragon is an aristocratic herb with a mild flavor and a hidden tang. It is excellent used in salad dressings and flavored vinegars. Add to poached fish, cooked vegetables, mustards, sauteed meats and even sugar cookies. Tarragon is indispensable for hollandaise and bearnaise sauces.

THYME

Thyme is a strong herb with a sweet fragrance. It adds a fine flavor to marinades, eggs, tomato sauces, chowders, meats and poultry, pasta, rice dishes and especially mushrooms, tomatoes and potatoes. Use lemon thyme in fish and poultry dishes.

TURMERIC

Turmeric root is a member of the ginger family. Once peeled, it is bright yellow in color. Turmeric is more commonly found and used in powdered form. It is often used in place of saffron, more for it's color than flavor which is musky, warm and peppery. Turmeric is most often used in curries, but is also used in chutneys, poultry, relishes, pickles, eggs, rice and vegetable dishes.

Metric Conversion Chart

VOLUME MEASUREMENTS (DRY)

$^1/_8$ teaspoon = 0.5 mL
$^1/_4$ teaspoon = 1 mL
$^1/_2$ teaspoon = 2 mL
$^3/_4$ teaspoon = 4 mL
1 teaspoon = 5 mL
1 tablespoon = 15 mL
2 tablespoons = 30 mL
$^1/_4$ cup = 60 mL
$^1/_3$ cup = 75 mL
$^1/_2$ cup = 125 mL
$^2/_3$ cup = 150 mL
$^3/_4$ cup = 180 mL
1 cup = 250 mL
2 cups = 1 pint = 500 mL
3 cups = 750 mL
4 cups = 1 quart = 1 L

VOLUME MEASUREMENTS (FLUID)

1 fluid ounce (2 tablespoons) = 30 mL
4 fluid ounces (1/2 cup) = 125 mL
8 fluid ounces (1 cup) = 250 mL
12 fluid ounces (1 1/2 cups) = 375 mL
16 fluid ounces (2 cups) = 500 mL

WEIGHTS (MASS)

$^1/_2$ ounce = 15 g
1 ounce = 30 g
3 ounces = 90 g
4 ounces = 120 g
8 ounces = 225 g
10 ounces = 285 g
12 ounces = 360 g
16 ounces = 1 pound = 450 g

OVEN TEMPERATURES

Fahrenheit	=	Celsius
200-205	=	95
220-225	=	105
245-250	=	120
275	=	135
300-305	=	150
325-330	=	165
345-350	=	175
370-375	=	190
400-405	=	205
425-430	=	220
445-450	=	230
470-475	=	245
500	=	260

CONVERSION FORMULAS

When you know	then multiply	To Determine
teaspoons	5.0	milliliters
tablespoons	15.0	milliliters
fluid ounces	30.0	milliliters
cups	0.24	liters
pints	0.47	liters
quarts	0.95	liters

WEIGHT

When you know	then multiply	To Determine
ounces	28.0	grams
pounds	0.45	kilograms

"Heart Healthy" Recipe Substitutions

ORIGINAL INGREDIENT	ALTERNATIVE
1 egg	2 egg whites = 1 egg or: $\frac{1}{4}$ cup egg substitute ie, Eggbeaters®, Second Nature® or Healthy Choice® Cholesterol-Free Egg Product. These items can be found in the frozen food or dairy section of your grocery store.
1 cup butter	$\frac{1}{2}$ to 1 cup margarine (liquid, soft or soft stick types). Use diet margarine when possible.
1 cup shortening	Can substitute $\frac{3}{4}$ cup oil in cookies, breads, etc. The product will be crispier. In some dessert products, equal amounts of applesauce can be substituted. This works best in cakes, muffins and quick breads.
1 cup whole milk	1 cup skim or 1% fat milk
1 cup cream	1 cup evaporated skim milk
1 cup shredded cheese	$\frac{1}{2}$ to 1 cup lower fat cheese such as part-skim mozzarella or (Alpine Lace®, Kraft® Free) or: $\frac{1}{4}$ cup very sharp cheese or: mix $\frac{1}{2}$ cup low fat cottage cheese with $\frac{1}{2}$ cup lower fat or regular cheese for casseroles
1 cup mayonnaise	1 cup non-fat or low-fat yogurt or: $\frac{3}{4}$ cup plain low-fat yogurt mixed with $\frac{1}{4}$ cup or less low-fat mayonnaise or: 1 cup low-calorie imitation, lite or fat-free mayonnaise (Kraft® Free mayonnaise, Weight Watcher® Fat Free)
1 cup sour cream	1 cup plain non-fat or low-fat yogurt (do not boil or it will curdle) or: Light N' Lively® Free, Viva® Light or Land O'Lakes® No-Fat
1 oz. baking chocolate	3 tablespoons cocoa powder plus 1 tablespoon oil
1 pound ground beef	1 pound extra lean grade (7% fat) ground beef or: Select a lean cut of beef and have it ground for you note: Use $\frac{1}{4}$ pound or less per person and drain the fat after cooking. If ground beef is browned before adding to a sauce or casserole, you can rinse it in a colander with hot water and lose more fat, but not nutrients. When using ground chicken or turkey, be sure to ask for ground chicken or turkey BREAST.

Courtesy of McKay Dee Hospital
Intermountain Health Care
Cardiac Fitness Institute

Index

Notes:

Notes:

Notes:

Notes:

Order Information
JLO ART OF COOKING

JUNIOR LEAGUE OF OGDEN
Women building better communities

2580 Jefferson Avenue • Ogden, Utah 84401
Office: 801-393-2540 • Fax: 801-392-5295
www.juniorleagueofogden.org

Thank you for your order! Proceeds from the sale of JLO Art of Cooking will be returned to the community through the training of volunteers and the development of community projects.

Order Date _____

Ship to: [　] Please check if billing address is different than shipping address.

_____
Name   Telephone

_____
Street Address

_____
City   State   Zip

Sold To: (If different than shipping address)

_____
Name   Telephone

_____
Street Address   Email Address

_____
City   State   Zip

Please send me _____ copies of JLO Art of Cooking @ $24.95 each $ _____

Postage and Handling @ $4.00 each $ _____

Total $ _____

Methods of Payment: [　] Mastercard   [　] Visa
                       [　] Check payable to JLO Publications

_____
Account Number   Expiration Date

_____
Cardholder Name

_____
Signature

Please allow 4 weeks for delivery
Photocopies will be accepted.